LOST AND FOUND IN SAN FRANCISCO

LOST AND FOUND IN SAN FRANCISCO

by

Emmett Shields

IN MEMORY OF RANDY SHILTS

ISBN: 1-58721-168-8

1stbooks - rev.07/5/00

About The Book

My first view of San Francisco was from an Oakland ferry. Literally and figuratively, I was a babe in the woods and the City became a finishing school for the young man fresh from the weeds of East Texas where, unfortunately, he was born.

In San Francisco, I began to shake the husk from my ears and the sand from my feet and to recognize that the only Texans one should know are those who escape. Firstly, I rejected all that I had been taught and commenced to recreate my self into the myth of my liking. I reveled in the arts, I learned to love opera, I learned to eat and to cook haute cuisine of many cultures. I learned, also, to luxuriate in the arms of many lovers. I was another version of Pygmalion and Baghdad by the Bay became my mentor.

This book is not just my story, it is a take on all the lonely young men who came to the City in search of their nirvana. In this book, I have tried to give a taste of what it was like to live in San Francisco before the plague…better known as AIDS.

Emmett Shields

For Monika Gierz, my favorite psychiatrist.

TABLE OF CONTENTS

1.

Modeling is tedious work and most especially so in an art class where one does it in the nude. As an established male in the business I work au naturel and have learned to wrap myself in a psychological cocoon which helps me get through a boring hour. I pay as little attention as possible to our dingy instructor and even less to her fledgeling Picassos unless I chance to spot a toothesome morsel among them.

I sat on an ancient piano stool, one of the circular kind which I associate with the jazz age with tassles of a faded rose hue, wondering what this bizarre setting meant to our instructor as I shivered from the cold and dampness of the loft which will forever smell of human sweat, a leftover from myriad ballet classes.

Ms. Reaves flirted with a reluctant forty and worked for the Adult Education Program who also pays my fee. She is a natural born drear and I had given her scant attention until the day she brought a baton to class, which seemed odd as an art class has nothing in common with an orchestra, but when our Ms. Reaves commenced to touch my flesh with the stick, the ghost of Freud came to the fore and I sensed that the wood was her way of fondling my body parts vicariously while pretending to talk about body musculature.

Reaves hair was mousy brown, she disdained makeup and jewelry and sheathed herself in shapeless dresses that were periodless in their bad taste. I categorized her as the type who takes perverse pride in her dowdiness which meant to me that she was a time-bomb ticking.

These occurrences made me cognizant of her seething passion for my body and I could not help but recoil when near her. Why is it that we cringe from unwanted lust being thrown our way by an undesirable creature when we can drool over an object of our selection, one who finds us equally repugnant? I'd ask Dr. Freud but he's no longer taking calls.

Ms. Reaves wore a wedding band so one assumed that she had a husband with whom she cohabited in some manner or form. Was he a lousy lover, a sadistic creep, a rabbit who left her unsatisfied? Did she despise him; did her flesh crawl from his? Not necessarily. Who would know better than I the complexities of human sexuality, the longing of the repressed, passion out of control? I might not understand the subject in terms suitable to Freud but mine were equally authentic as they came from the sexual arena. I was self-taught on and by the streets.

Some say that we cannot be in love with more than one person at a time. Empirical data from the archives of my existence deny the validity of this hypothesis unless I am the exception that proves the rule. Who could know better than I that she could be in love with her husband while lusting for another, in this case, a naked model, and that said lust could make hamburger of her innards because mine have scar tissue to prove the point. The lady was strangling with lust for my flesh and what she got or didn't get at home was of little consequence as I sat on that stool with Goosebumps showing. Her mind was lost in a swirling fog of passion, her vision had become opaque and she was confused to the point where she was incapable of knowing lust from love from obsession and would end up calling them love when all three have their different meanings.

It was at this point that I wanted to get free from her and the inevitable explosion by requesting another assignment. But if I did, I would surely be asked why. Advising my superior that the instructor had the hots for my body would most likely backfire leaving me as the villain of the piece.

I would have given the matter scant attention had Ms. Reaves refrained from touching my anatomy with the baton but in Freudian terms, this was her way of caressing me without actually touching which gave her a certain safety in numbers by doing it before the class as if it were part of instruction when any dolt would recognize the change in her voice timbre, that her face grew flushed and that she became erratic when touching those body parts where she wished to emphasize musculature to her students, so it seemed, but in reality, her's was a ruse for caressing my body parts with the baton, the buttocks, abdomen and thighs in particular, while coming as close to the groin as her slight hold on reality would allow. Clearly, I had need to get rid of Ms. Reaves before she got rid of me by losing the last of her self-control and attacking me before the class.

On the last day that I modeled for her class, I recalled my first obsession for the flesh of another which occurred during my freshman year of college. I was swept into the vortex of madness and confusion with symptoms of both love and hate for the same person and some brain once said that there is a thin line between the two. The passion that consumed me made me want to destroy with passion that individual for whom my lust burned. Now I was on the receiving end and even if I were stupid enough to take this crazed creature she would ultimately destroy herself and me as the gossamer strands between love and hate were erased. Conversely, if I continued to ignore her, she might attack me before the class. I felt premonitions from her hot breath on my neck, back and arms, and when she ran the baton through my pubic hairs it took all of my will power to keep from recoiling. Even so, eyebrows were raised and sardonic smiles appeared among the students who were onto her little game. Fortunately, the bell rang before Ms. Reaves lost her total cool and dissolved into a psychotic puddle and whatever happened, she would blame me. In this case, the cliche saved by the bell had much validity. I put on my robe, slipped into my zoris and made my way toward the men's dressing room. As my hand touched the knob, I heard her feather steps behind me before she spoke in that breathlessly apologetic voice that I have grown to despise.

"Mr. Stone, please, a word with you. It seems to me that you are showing a marked disinterest in your job. I felt it my duty to call the matter to your attention. Perhaps a little more joie de vivre." She made her twitching grimaces that pass for smiles while twisting the lapels of her coat.

Angered by her desperate charade, I said: "Ms. Reaves, a model is nothing but a hunk of flesh to be studied and drawn by a group of students. Just as a cadaver is to be dismembered by doctors of the future. Both model and cadaver perform their jobs in total silence and with utmost discretion. You will excuse me. I should like to take a hot shower.

"But it does seem,' she rattled on, refusing to let go. Strictly by impulse, I let my kimono fall open as I told the lady, "It's yours, if you want it, but I don't come cheap." She choked on shock and as I entered the dressing room I heard her scream.

I luxuriated under the hot jets from the shower and wondered if she would dare appear at the next class, or would I receive a summons to answer whatever tale of woe she might concoct. As the sting of the spray brought relaxation, I went back to my desperate collegiate affair and recalled my voracious appetite for the flesh of another which assumed cannibalistic proportions. Succinctly put, this type of passion is too hot not to cool down ... thank you, Cole Porter.. and the day finally came when my love object became strangled by my insatiable appetite. Perhaps it was karmic that I found myself on the other end of the spectrum, the object of Ms. Reaves' monstrous appetite for my flesh. Gasping for air, during the college contretemps, I heard words that I had never heard before, words new to my ears but old to my soul. Said my collegiate fantasy, "Somebody has to win out in these things. To hear what I felt for another referred to as a thing was high blasphemy and stung as would a hive of angry bees. With a primal scream, I crossed a threshold from which there is no return. The mirror to my innocence had been cracked, naivete lay in shards while I was left naked to shiver from my wounds. Now I had done the same thing to Ms. Reaves as I heard her primal scream echo down the corridor. Alas, there is no kind way to jolt the lust from another back into reality without trauma. Soothing words will only make the quagmire more treacherous. I shrugged. It was done. I was resigned to looking for another job while Ms. Reaves choked on my bone in her throat, metaphorically speaking.

I heard sirens faintly in the distance as I completed my shower on the fifth floor and imagined that police and firemen were coming to rescue me from a predatory female.

I was sitting on a towel spread on a bench when the door to the showers was flung open by a young stud with a mop of blond curls and an ass at least one-third too large for his stocky frame. He wore a gleaming new blue uniform of the SFPD which indicated that he was a rookie first day out to scare the public.

4

To advertise the obvious, he waved his drawn pistol in various directions, and by pistol I do not refer to the ample providence given to him by nature and genes, I refer to the steel new piece from departmental supply now waving in the wind from the hands of a novice cop. Freeze!" he cried, as his metallic equipment seemed to burn his hands.

"Thank you, Officer," I responded, "As a model for the art class, I have already frozen my buns from an hour on a stool. Now I am relaxing after a long stay under a scalding shower."

His thought processes were as obvious as a computer printout which could be read on his baby blues. "The art teacher was found nude on the roof, waving a stick with which she had been doing naughty things, all the while threatening to jump, and I'm supposed to search the premises."

"Officer, I had nothing to do with the instructor parading nude on the roof," I lied, with sincerety. "I've worked with her for a couple of months and my non-professional opinion is that the broad is nuts, off her rocker, sex-starved and subject to aberrant behavior. Did she jump?"

"No. Two cops on the roof managed to snare her in a net before she took a dive."

"Pity you didn't arrive earlier," I lamented. "One look at you and she would have gone over the Golden Gate in a state of ecstasy."

"What do you mean by that?" he asked, highly suspicious.

"She would have gone ape over your frame. May I lower my hands now, please."

"Yeah," he advised, not quite sure whether or not he had been flattered. "But don't try anything cute. And why are you sitting up here naked?"

"I am undressed as I have just finished a shower. My suggestion is that you take the next modeling class in my place, in which case, you'll understand. With that overly-developed body of yours, the bulging biceps and box, I have no doubt but what all the female students will be wet between their thighs while all the males will sport erections."

Outraged, the Officer waved his weapon in my direction and snarled, "You are an obscene pervert!"

5

"Thank you, Officer. I am most pleased by your analysis?"

"I'm leaving here now," he informed, "And you get dressed. Come to think of it, I want your name, address and telephone number. You must be guilty of something."

When dressed and ready to depart, I walked down to the elevator for a short ride to the roof. Once there, I walked around the parapet looking down for some clue to recent events but there were none. One might assume that Ms. Reaves was snug in her straitjacket or tethered to her bed or shot full of valium. As I traversed the parapet, I remembered Humpty Dumpty and One Flew Over the Cuckoo's Nest. But I'm in San Francisco, I paused to remember, where there is always one more in line waiting for their twenty seconds of fame as they leap off the Golden Gate bridge.

2.

As I walked down McAllister toward the Hyde Street cable I kept reviewing words said by Camus: that the desire for possession is inevitable to the point that it can survive even love itself, a condition of human behavior that I had to believe. Choked by lust, we fixate upon the current idol of our fantasy and call it reality when in fact we are in a state of delusion. Pity the poor souls who cannot lech for the sheer joy of leeching. Praise be, that was never my problem although I did need breathing space from time to time so that I might slip *away* and lick my wounds as would the animal who has been bested in a struggle for a bitch in heat.

Yet even in the agony of defeat, I knew that I would do it again. All that was needed was an ego-ideal, a fantasy to feed the delusion. Tortured by lust, obsession and delusion one may wonder where love begins and insanity takes over. I don't know what my psychiatrist would have to say on this subject but I shall speak of it during our next session.

Once more, I thought about my collegiate obsession and how it had changed me forever as I wanted to destroy with passion that individual for whom my lust burned.

Most appalling was the discovery that I was made of sterner stuff than previously thought and as I pulled the daggers from my heart, melodramatically speaking, I commenced to die a little each day smug in the knowledge that I would ultimately recover. Someone had to win. I had been told. Then let it be me. From this source I met the horrible within me which shocked more than all else for I knew that whatever the cost I would not be the loser. I suppose that I met myself on that fateful day and didn't like what I saw.

These were the stepping stones that took me to San Francisco there to grow up and where I evidenced much in common with Ferdinand the Bull, a cartoon character who had to sniff all the lillies in the field and in the City by the Bay life is one giant florist shop. As one grew and blossomed forth one learned that in San Francisco the season lasts forever. Paris may have its spring... tra la.. but in Baghdad by the Bay there is an eternal primavera.

Discretion's and inhibitions were tossed to the wind as carelessly as restaurants along the Wharf toss mountains of leftovers to the squalling gulls. Conquest by conquest, orgasm by orgasm, one's emotional and physical endurance were tested on a daily basis. Drowning in lust and delusions one went as mad as a child in See's Candy Store or as an adult reacting to the symphony of exotic smells from David's Kosher Deli. One could not eat without staring into the eyes of one's next meal.

Questions as vital as the following regulated one's existence. Would the day be devoted singularly to the pursuits of the flesh or could one find time to do one's laundry between sex in the afternoon and sex after dinner. Would there be a matinee of the latest Broadway hit at the Curran theatre followed by cocktails at the Mark. Would there be an evening performance of Salome at the Opera House followed by flamenco at a club on Broadway, or would one be privy to the genius of a young comic on his way up the ladder to stardom. And after two o'clock of the morn, when the bars must close, would one luck into an orgy in some fancy pad on Telegraph Hill.

Would one cruise Fisherman's Wharf after a morning of modeling Macy's latest fashions for the Sunday edition, mean and sticky from working under hot lights.

Drugs were around, drugs have always been around, but they were not yet a problem for the bourgeoisie for we were high on life. Needles were redundant. The worst we ever got was a case of syphilis while gonorrhea was first cousin to a misplaced head cold. Penicillin was a fact and a blessing from World War II and would cure anything, unless one were allergic to it, so our doctors told us, and so we believed in the omnipotence of our naivete, knowing not of things to come.

Every three months, I would sell a pint of blood at the Irwin Memorial Blood Bank for twenty-five dollars and a free shot of bourbon. I was a professional donor for St. Francis Hospital, thanks to a friend who was secretary to the resident pathologist. These were my primary sources of income before the modeling class. I took the modeling job in the drafty loft which smelled of human sweat and shook a lot for twenty-five dollars an hour while sitting nude on a stool. I weighed one -hundred and fifty pounds, more or less, and the bone structure of a six-footer was readily apparent. These were my primary sources of income while I lived well on the generosity of a sex-starved older generation who were ready and willing to pay.

I shared a pad and in those days living was easy in San Francisco and I thought nothing of climbing sixty-six steps from Jackson Street to the third-floor billiard room which I called home. Part of my ritual was to put on my Belgian cord of midnight blue with vest, bow tie and hankie artfully folded. With topcoat, gloves and hat, I would sally forth on an August evening, the coldest time of the year in the City by the Bay. I welcomed any cloud in the sky which gave me an excuse to carry my umbrella, a most handy prop. On these occasions, I always made my entrance through the revolving doors of the Fairmont through which kings and queens, the famous and the infamous have passed. I would work the posh bars of the Hotel where wealthy men and women shopped for an attractive young man who would escort them to Carmel for the weekend, or a fortnight in Honolulu, a few days in Las Vegas or a sojourn in Cuernavaca. I had the social graces, the aura of the well bred, I had the education which included two years of drama school which trained me well in the art of selling. I had a head of golden blond hair when bleached by the sun. And I could read a menu in French with better accent than understanding. Maybe all this sounds exciting to the lonely young man in Kansas with dreams in his eyes and an abundance of semen but to me there was something missing although I did not know what it was, which may be why I ran from marriage to the daughter of affluent French refugees.

Their daughter worshiped me, or thought she did, but now I know that she would have adored anyone who would put up with her. She was emotionally starved and bled me as would a plague of leeches and each time that we had sex she ran to her gynecologist to have her vagina adjusted. According to her, the organ turned over during the act of sex. To this day, I do not understand why a vagina would flip over during the act of copulation. In my mad mind I associate such phenomena with the flipping of flapjacks. Then there was her personal hygiene which grew to be her friends' problem as well. At times, we found it necessary to throw her in the shower and bar the door. Perhaps she feared that she might miss something.

I had more in common with her father who had been a practicing psychiatrist in Paris before the Germans came. He spoke little English and thought completely in French, while I spoke a little French and thought completely in English but our communication did not depend upon verbiage. I have always thought that Pere and I would have gotten along well had we been left alone. Mere was as charming as an over cured dill which might have been the result of the fact that she did not have the pedigree of Pere who picked her from the Comedie Francais or one such enterprise. Madame had a horse face and looked down her nose at me while I returned the favor. At other times, she would pretend that I wasn't there which made for exhausting weekends. Mere had delusions of grandeur and thought that her daughter should marry someone like Gregory Peck. Daughter's greatest coup was having been deflowered by a prominent actor when she was sweet sixteen, as the song goes. I must have been insane to have walked out on all that money in Swiss banks but character had nothing to do with it.

While I dressed the part when necessary, I wasn't really fond of San Francisco high style. Early on, in my days there, I learned that what I had to sell, trade or give to charity was most marketable in a pair of scruffy sneakers, dirty jeans and sweatshirt plus a two-day growth of beard. It was difficult to make my way through a supermarket without exchanging dates with one or two hungry souls. I didn't know it yet but I was a budding rebel, all bourgeoisie on the surface but confused at the core.

During those days, I played Ferdinand the Bull to the hilt and dallied with numerous ladies of surface quality with flush checking accounts. They were divorcees, mistresses and widows and mostly they were bored housewives with whom I shared picnics in the park, walks underneath the Golden Gate Bridge, or across it as it sang and swayed attesting to its aliveness. One should not die without having walked across the Bridge and there were occasions when I thought about jumping as a way out of an undesirable liaison between the sheets.

Aquarians are alleged to be blessed or cursed with the qualities of the chameleon. Our moods switch easily and we shed our colors with ease. Perhaps that is why I moved through different social strata with elan. A pharmacist buddy of mine worked in the wild little town of Winnemucca, Nevada which sported three legal bordellos situated across the railroad tracks, of course, a social cliche for sure. My pal supplied the girls with their drug needs and the accouterment of their trade and was looked upon as a friend rather than a potential customer. I spent two consecutive New Year Eves in those houses which gave me the goofy idea that I should rent a room in my favorite of the three where I could live and write while doing my version of Toulousse la Trec with legs.

It was during this period that I learned to avoid unwanted seductions by talking them to death. Discarding gay patois for Webster pure, this was the period when I tried to go straight but to no avail. The Puritan Protestant work ethic raised feelings of guilt because I wasn't a young executive climbing the corporate ladder while being bored to death. That was long before I gave up guilt for Lent and subsequently forever. These were the days when I was perfecting the duplicity that would *codify* my life until the day when there was nothing left to be duplicitous about. I was perfecting my myth although I didn't know it. I was a rebel with a cause who wanted to live the hedonist's dream of a lifetime crammed with sensations, giving lip service to the establishment as an outlaw to the order, an outsider trying to be all that he loathed. I took a few more years before I came to accept that I was the myth and the myth was I.

I thought of Camus again as I walked along McAllister to the Hyde cable which would take me home to my mistress' elegant flat on Russian Hill. The Frenchman says that the desire for possession is inevitable to the point that it can survive even love itself and his words seemed to describe perfectly Ms. Reaves and her most recent behavior. Choked by lust, we fixate upon the current idol of our fantasies and... in her case... it was I. .and call it reality when in fact we are in a state of delusion. Some of us poor souls must always believe that we are in love in order to enjoy sex and how exhausting that must be.

Harking back to the agony of my college affair and the pain of that defeat, I knew that I would do it again. All that was needed was the ego-ideal, the fantasy to feed the delusion. Tortured by lust, obsession and delusion one may wonder where love begins and madness takes over, which brings to mind Confucius and one of his memorable quotes: love is a soul sickness to be gotten over as quickly as possible. Adding a postscript to the gentleman's words, as I turned to admire a curvaceous ass swing from port to starboard with the accuracy of a metronome, I postscripted accordingly: one should get over love as quickly as possible so that one can do it all over again. Another riddle for my psychiatrist as I made a mental note to speak to her about it on my next visit.

Someone had to win in affairs of the heart. I had been told Then let it be me. Perhaps Ms. Reaves met herself on that fateful day when she was caught in a net with the baton strategically placed, a matter over which I had no control. No telephone calls, no police visits, no arrests, no inquisitions, only a certain askew study of my face by my mistress which could easily be the result of my overly-active paranoia.

All things being equal, I reported for art class on the following Tuesday. Much to my surprise, Absalom Prevet, Professor Emeritus, Department of Art, University of California, Berkeley campus, was there to greet me. The Professor was head of the department during my first and sophomore year at Cal and it was he who picked me green from a long line of hopefuls to take off my clothes and to show the world what I had to offer. Apparently, he was more than satisfied as it was he who started me on the road to nowhere as a nude model. Once, I asked the Prof what was the reason for my selection and I was told that I was chosen because I shed my wearing apparel faster than anyone else.

Skaken with delight and yet haunted by a premonition, I gushed, "To what do we owe the presence of your eminence, Professor Prevet?"

"Visi d'arte, visi d'amore," he sang, off-key. "So you're the walking erection that drove la Reaves out of her mind. I should have known."

"Why, Doctor," I protested, but not too convincingly, "I have no idea what you mean."

"Don't play coy with me, Stone. You're a phallic symbol and you know it. Why else would I have picked you out of a long line of hopefuls that fateful day during your first term at Cal. From what I've read and heard," he declared, indicating the roll of white paper in front of which I was to sit, "The lady known as Reaves didn't need much encouragement to do herself in."

As I sat, Professor Prevet presented me with a copy of the morning Chronicle artfully folded for my edification, and as I sat, I saw a photograph of myself sitting nude whilst Ms. Reaves poked at my private parts with her baton. "Oh, God!" I cried, as I glanced about the room to find all eyes turned heavenward as if they had just taken a vow of piety. One of the scruffy wretches had caught the scene perfectly with a private camera and after financial barter, so I assumed, the negatives were sold to the paper. Now, as I sat with the evidence in hand, not one of the monsters would look me eye to eye. Accusingly, I glared at the Professor who declared, "One of our sneaky little beasts is a damned good photographer. Stone," he intoned, "I must declare that you have never let me down. Seeing as how it was you, my most eminent model, who got us into this mess, I volunteered to teach the class. It was my artistic duty," the Professor announced, swelling with pride. "God knows what trouble you'll get us into next with that innocent face of yours and I wouldn't miss it for a pot of gold."

Obviously, the Professor was as happy with the situation as I was not. As I read the lushy gush from the morning press I didn't turn red, I was too tanned for that. If anything, I blanched a bit. Everyone knew, as of the morning edition, my mistress included. The thought of explanations exhausted me while the Professor was having the day of his life. Inspired by events, he devoted the entire hour to the drawing of male genitalia which kept me exposed throughout the allotted time. While I had nothing to feel guilty about I was nevertheless branded as the villain of the piece according to the Chronicle. As I read on, I discovered that Ms. Reaves was indeed netted with the baton protruding from her private part. Audaciously, the article suggested that I may have been giving Ms. Reaves lessons on the flute. One :thing I've always admired about the Chronicle is their raising of the doube entendre to a high art.

Watching the Professor perform during the art class rekindled my admiration for him. Had it not been for his assistance my struggle to get through Cal would have been difficult at best. Once ensconced, Dr. Prevet saw that I had all the modeling work I could handle and was quite adept at playing pimp on my behalf. His diversified efforts alleviated most of the collegiate strain, financially speaking.

"Thank God, you're young and physically healthy and have an infinite capacity for orgasms," Doc exclaimed, "And if you should die of penis exhaustion, I'll make sure that you're buried with a permanent erection. What an epitaph it will make: rest in piece, eternal erection."

I moved back to San Francisco after receiving my Master's degree and shared a pad with a friend and in those days living was easy until I met my mistress and was taken in by her as a course of least resistance. She required her sexual fulfillment, opened a joint bank account and other than showing me off at fashion shows I was left to my own devises. I caught on early to her pleasure in finding me in the press for some peccadillo which seemed to enhance her reputation and following such occasions, my presence with her in public increased until the novelty waned. She was immensely pleased with the art class caper and wore me down with public appearances.

3.

Art classes were packed after the <u>incident</u> and some of my notoriety apparently rubbed off on the ballet class as well. Students of the dance commenced to enter the rehearsal hall before our hour was finished in order to catch a glimpse of the naked ogre who had driven the poor art teacher insane. Professor Prevet was delirious with joy over such sudden interest in the artistic muse while his most infamous model sulked.

On one such occasion, I took notice of a raven-haired ballerina who had arrived early. She stood at the practice bar with right foot on the metal and with right cheek touching her knee. From this traditional exercise position she grinned as I put on my robe and tied the cord about my waist. Irked by her audacity at this intrusion and the viewing of my body without pay, I remained aloof from her wide grin. I disliked her intensely, which I should have recognized as a prelude to disaster but didn't, as she continued to view me free of charge. Secondarily, I am not fond of black curly hair pulled back and held in place by a kerchief. Over her exercise togs, she wore a sweatshirt which did little to enhance the human frame as only ballerinas in tights turn me on. Garbed in a heavy shirt in the cool and damp of the loft, I concluded that she might be short and dumpy which gave me further excuse for disliking her.

Finally, impertinently, she spoke. "Do you do this often?" Her inflections made me feel that I had been caught mugging old ladies on Polk Street.

In my most clipped English, I said, "I only sell my body on Tuesdays and Thursdays and you haven't paid your fee." I was increasingly nettled by God knows what.

"Then I shall change my class schedule," she remarked, suppressing a giggle.

She was giving me the business, in a manner of speaking, this I knew. Hers was the classic come-on, a tease and perhaps an invitation and if not then her goal was to create that impression in order to get me hot and bothered so that I would pursue her, in which case, she could rebuff me and win our

15

match of wits. In short, we were engaged in a primeval form of sexual chess. Deciding that I did not wish to be a pawn, I slipped into my zoris and departed for the dressing room without another glance in her direction.

I indulged in a scalding shower primarily to warm my bones and when dried, dressed and ready to depart, I walked the long way around to the wooden elevator, the freight kind that has a door which opens vertically. As I turned the corner the ballerina was leaning against the wooden frame to the lift. Jerking myself together, I asked, "What happened to your class?"

"I decided that I'd rather play with you," she explained, as she twirled her hands in saucy exercise movements. "Shall we go somewhere Italian for cappuccino?"

"I'm afraid that my schedule is full for the day," I lied.

"So is mine. We're dancing Die Fledermaus tonight and we really get a workout in the second act with all that can-can stuff. I love it. Do you love opera?"

"I practically live at the Opera House during season."

"What are your favorites?"

"Anything except Verdi. He's too um pah pah for my tastes."

"My name is Xanae," she informed, as we hit the street. "It's Greek."

"Obviously."

"That's bitchy of you."

"And you have about thirteen brothers who fish and your parents have been here for years and can't speak a word of English."

"Only six," she corrected. "My father is dead and you're right, mother refuses to learn English. She wants to go home to our island and starve to death."

"What happened to your father?"

"In a jealous rage, his mistress cut his throat." She spoke glibly while making a sign of the cross in memory of her dead parent.

"Not knowing whether to believe her or not, I asked, "Are you legal?"

"I'm twenty-one. Want to see my driver's license?"

16

Feeling foolish, I replied, "That won't be necessary. How old are your six brothers?" I inquired, trying not to shudder at the thought of such a progeny.

Raising her eyes heavenward and counting on her fingers, she replied, "Twenty-three to thirty."

"And you are the baby sister."

"Yes. And my mother thinks that I shall die and go to hell for being a dancer."

Amused, in spite of myself, I said, "Tell your mother that only bad dancers go to hell."

"She wouldn't get it." Glancing at her watch as we approached her red sports model, she exclaimed, "It's ten past eleven and already I'm starving. Why not skip cappuccino and have lunch. There's a little Greek cafe in the Mission that does delicious gyros."

"I'm not driving," I explained.

"I'll take you home," she volunteered, and then gasped. "Forget the gyros. My brothers are not fishing today and they eat there often. Today is not the day to explain you."

"Today is not the day that I wish to be explained," I countered, as I had a vision of six hulking Greeks coming at me with knives.

"I have a key to a friend's apartment. I stay with her often. Why not skip lunch for bed."

"Anything to avoid your brothers. I have no desire to be given a third degree. Of course, I could tell them that you seduced me."

"They'd never believe you," she giggled, "Poor darlings, they think that I'm still a virgin."

I went to her friend's apartment, of course, in a building that overlooks the Broadway tunnel, where we tried to tear clothing from each other as lust blazed to full fury. I managed to stagger from the apartment in time to climb Russian hill to my mistress' flat where I stirred a meal and with all the charm of a born liar with a loose zipper, I waved a wooden spoon of affection in her direction as she arrived at six.

I spent a restless night, mostly in the living room where I sipped Courvoisier and watched the fog do its magic on the Bay.

At breakfast, my mistress declared, "You were restless last night. Was it indigestion or inspiration?"

"I'm not sure," I replied, "Most likely, a bit of both."

During the morning hours, I sat by the window and tried to come to terms with my passing encounter with the precocious ballerina. My hands shook, I choked on air, my eyes commenced to glaze, I had palpitations which are a form of panic, all of it more than enough to drive a hypochondriac like myself to the nearest emergency. Finally, I was able to articulate my condition by recalling words once said to me by a Sicilian friend who was the first and only person to explain the Italian Thunderclap, and as this recall began so did my understanding of my dilemma:

I had been struck. In case an explanation is needed, the Thunder clap is the all-consuming curse of falling hopelessly and senselessly in love. The Thunderclap is not a state of being, it is a disease of the soul.

In contradiction to this devastating passion I saw myself as being forced to leave my mistress comfy pad for some cheap apartment where I could be alone with the ballerina, which would involve her ability to evade her family and my adroitness at staying clear of her six irate brothers. Whatever the problems…real or imagined…I was suddenly mad about all things Greek: food, wine, dance and flesh.

At one o'clock of the afternoon, I grabbed my windbreaker and made my way down Russian Hill toward Broadway and the tunnel…now thought of the tunnel of love…while I hummed bits of Rogers and Hammerstein such as: hello, young lovers, whoever you are. I rang the buzzer and there was an instant response. I climbed the three flights of stairs in a rush. I knocked and the door was opened instantly. Her hair was down about her shoulders and fresh from the shower she was swathed in a dampened robe. Her eyes grew misty. I grabbed her with a ferocity heretofore unknown to me and kissed her as we moved as one toward the bed. The curse was mutual as each of us tried to eat the other alive. Again, I heard Rogers and Hammerstein's lyrics…hello, young lovers, I hope your troubles are few.

Sated, for awhile, I looked into her eyes and from some part of me that was still sane, I knew that her commitment was greater than mine and this frightened me deeply. Pity the poor Anglo who gets involved with Greeks because they still live out their great tragedies in the flesh of their day. Greeks should live only with Greeks, I decided, but by then I was too far gone to act on such a perception.

She was a member of the Corps de ballet of the San Francisco Company and had six brothers who would remove my parts one at a time without anesthesia if they discovered that their sister was no longer a virgin. Such a joke it was, a scary joke, their myth of her virginity as she was about as sexually active as I.

For several weeks, we met at her friends apartment, we had trysts in her car, in dark stairwells, in cheap motels and her arrivals at the ballet bar five minutes before my art class was finished placed me in a perilous position as I fought to suppress an erection before my students which would definitely destroy my professional qualification as an artist's model. This state of affairs went on with a careless abandon fed by passion which is hard to hide, in particular, from a mistress who is keeping you in her elegant flat on Russian Hill.

The denouement was inevitable and finally on a fog-swept Sunday, mistress put down the Chronicle for a moment and said, with a cold smile, "You're having an affair."

"Yes! No!" I cried, wringing my hands. "I don't know what it is."

"I don't mind your sexual escapades," she reassured me, "As long as there's something left for our boudoir. But of late, darling, I have been sadly neglected. At this very moment, you are a caged lion, a dog who knows there's a bitch in heat in the next apartment. Try and pull yourself together. Incidentally, we're invited to an open house at Selena's on Friday. She's insane with jealousy at having been dropped from your list and practically licks my hand, although I don't know what she expects from me, unless I act the role of a pimp on her behalf. Or should that be pimpette! I accepted her invitation. It's a divine chance to see her suffer and now, there's a bonus, I will

19

be able to see the two of you suffer together.   Life has its moments."

"You don't understand," I railed.

"Who is she, may I ask?"

"She's a ballerina, a member of the Corps."

"Oh, dear, she won't be able to keep you in the style to which you have become accustomed."

I hated her for her lack of empathy and in a bad moment I compounded my stupidity by making too many confessions as if I were a Catholic who can vomit his sins, get absolution and do it all over again.

"She's Greek and has six brothers," I moaned.

"My, my," said the amused one, "Is she good?"

"How dare you as me such a question!" I wailed.

"I was not speaking of sex. I was speaking of ballet and talent. Bye the bye, I'm flying to Los Angeles in the morning for several days of work. I'm sure you'll miss me terribly. I shall return in time for Selena's bash. I wouldn't miss it. Beware, darling, you're beginning to bore me."

Her threats did not go unheeded. I grabbed my cap and windbreaker and went for a walk. Need I say that I could be found at the stage door to the Opera House as Xanae emerged from a matinee performance of La Traviata, or La Triviata, as Mario loves to call it. She was shivering and under obvious distress as we walked toward a coffee shop, hand in hand.

"I told them," she said, as she stirred cream into her coffee.

"Told them what?" My kinetic response rattled spoons.

"My mother and my brothers that I was in love with you and that you were not responsible for the loss of my virginity and that they were to leave you alone. I told them that they could kill me, if they chose, but that they were to leave you alone. Mother fainted and tried to die. They have threatened to ship me to our island off the coast of Greece. Do what you want with me, I yelled, but you cannot stop me from loving him. It was all terribly exhausting as things Greek always are but, finally, we worked out a compromise of sorts. They want you to go out on the boat with them for a day, to find out what you're made of, so they put it."

"Me! On a fishing boat." I was shaken by such a bizarre suggestion. "I get sick in a bathtub."

She tried to giggle but was too emotionally distraught to be convincing. "Try it, love, try it for me."

How does one refuse the impossible when the eyes of one's beloved overflow with tears? I should have fled for my life and my sanity but the Thunderclap was stronger than what passed for brains. Fortunately, mistress mine was in Los Angeles; lies and evasions could be avoided temporarily.

The reluctant fisherman, the mortal coward arrived at the pier where the Xanae was at anchor. She was a handsome boat but I could not equate her with my ballerina. Sans preliminaries or greetings, the six brothers took me in charge and ill-fitted me in yellow plastic boots, pants, jacket and gloves after which they shoved a souwester on my head and tried to choke me as the hat was tied under my chin. Between each barked order, one or the other would curse me in Greek. They might not kill me but they were hell bent on giving me a bad time. As soon as we left harbor I became seasick and ran to the starboard side where I vomited on one of the brothers who was tending nets near the water line. At that moment, he was perilously close to using me for bait. He cursed me in Greek.

As we got out to sea and hit a fine school activity aboard became frenetic. As fish were dumped from nets onto the deck I was to shovel them into the hole. I fell and slid in fish slime and threw up on my catch as well as myself with Greek curses ringing in my ears and when they weren't cursing, they bruised me about all the while howling with glee. Once I almost threw myself down the hole intended for the fish. This agony continued until we docked around noon. As soon as I could get free of my plastic drag, I jumped ship and ran like a rabbit from a fire toward the main arterial where, luckily, I was able to hail a Yellow Cab.

"Russian Hill," I panted, as I got into the front seat with the driver.

"My God, how you stink," he exclaimed, emphasizing the obvious as he opened his window.

Once home and inside the flat, I opened all windows hoping that the brisk winds would pull the stench of fish from the premises. I threw my clothes into the washing machine, my ruined deck shoes down the garbage chute and then hopped into the shower for a prolonged scrub. While drying, I battened down the windows to protect me from fog-filled winds which were piercingly cold. I mixed a scotch and soda and thanked our maker for the fact that my mistress was still in Las Angeles and, hopefully, the smell of fish would be gone by the time of her return.

I commenced to call my ballerina, shuddering with each ring, and each time that I called, someone came on the line and cursed me in Greek before the line went dead. I knew her home address which was on the outer perimeter of the Mission District and thought of driving out but to what avail. The least that could happen was that I would be blasted with Greek curses while the worst might be a gunshot wound in some vital spot. Even limbs might be broken. I was paralyzed by fear and aching from loss. She would never call the flat, we had agreed on that.

I went to her ballet class on the following day but she wasn't there and her classmates had no information to give. Toward the end of my modeling class on Tuesday, the day afterward, I began to look in vain for her arrival. I slunk homeward, deep in a funk, to find that my mistress had returned.

We had little to say to one another as she spent most of her day on the phone with business acquaintances. About the only exchange of dialogue was to remind me of Selena's Friday night affair. The time between Tuesday and Friday didn't fly by, it crawled. On Friday afternoon, she suggested that I make myself presentable for the evening and with a bitchy postscript, she added, "If you can." I was definitely in the doghouse and it was growing smaller by the hour. We ate Chinese which had been brought in and then my mistress commenced her ritual of being fashionably late, a fetish that seemed to have its genesis in her position of power in the local fashion world. Personally, I find this sort of contrivance a bore but I was not in a position to antagonize the source of my calories. Also, I was limp from agony at my inability to contact Xanae.

We arrived fashionably late, whatever that may mean, and Selena slithered forward to greet us. The perfunctory pecks on cheeks were done with the usual duplicity, "So glad you could come," our hostess swooned, "Both of you," while withering me with a glance that made the hair on my neck quiver. "And how was Los Angeles, my dear, need I ask?" Selena dotes on being clever while lacking those necessary ingredients that make up wit and humor. "And did our dear boy behave himself while you were away?"

"I found Los Angeles rather pleasant for a few days," my mistress explained, lying through her capped front teeth.

Merciful Savior, I told myself, this is going to be a horrible scene, even worse than I imagined. Selena can scarcely contain herself. She knows about Xanae but how did she find out? She's salivating for her pound of flesh, she may even use me for soup meat. I feel it coming. Oh, why did you come to this ridiculous charade. The bitch has one talent and that's for fucking up the lives of whomever crosses her. By virtue of having been born a Flood, a far distant cousin of the famous pioneer family, nabobs who helped build the City, Selena manages to walk the fringes of society in an outcast sort of way. Why did I ever succumb to this dreadful beast? Surely, I was never that desperate. I'll blame it on Professor Prevet who conditioned me to drop my pants at the command to <u>heel</u>.

Selena coiled her way to other groups playing the hostess bit to the hilt while mistress and I played our parts as polite guests. Mistress gave the impression that she was slumming and I made a mental note to congratulate her when we got home, if I were allowed inside. Through it all, and from afar, I kept watch on our hostess who had some hidden reason to justify her state of ebullience and when I cast a wary eye in her direction, she would turn away, as if I might perceive the reason for her behavior. Which was a far cry from her usual slavering self when she would be hanging around my neck much in the manner of a friendly asp, which is probably an oxymoron, the words as well as the persona of whom I spoke.

My old Sicilian friend Mario, he who had introduced me to the Italian Thunderclap, joined me in a quiet alcove of the sprawling living room and it was I who brought up Selena's unusual behavior. "Is she high on something," I suggested.

"She sniffs and snorts, of course, and I've been told that she uses the needle in the groin but none in their right mind is going to investigate that nether region. Personally," friend continued, "I'd like to strangle her with my Italian sausage. Are you all right?" he asked, as he gave study to my apparently wan appearance. "You look as though you've given too much blood."

"I'm muddling through."

"Lunch?"

"Soon."

Time dragged its heels, the way a drag queen in spikes traverses Market Street after midnight, as I moved from group to group like amoebae changing forms. Exchanging shallow chat always with an eye for Selena who dallied conspicuously near the main entrance. For this reason, I was witness to the occasion as she opened the door in response to a bell that none could hear from where I was stationed. I don't think that I was much surprised when Xanae entered followed by a rising star of the San Francisco Ballet and a living Greek god, albeit pure Aryan. I recalled our previous meeting and that Erec was gay and destined for ballet stardom, and as Selena is one of San Francisco's most eminent fag hags she would obviously know Erec who would obviously know Xanae. Thus was the mystery solved. With each in hand, she moved in the direction of my mistress and, at the same time, I moved toward her, too, as if I could protect her when, in reality, I was trying to protect myself.

"Darlings," Selena drooled, "This is Xanae Constontatos and Erec Berg of the Ballet. You know Tom, of course."

Erec recalled our earlier meeting and we shook hands with genuine warmth. He was oblivious to Selena's vicious little scheme while Xanae was shocked at our meeting. Mistress took the entire vignette with finesse and without a flutter of her lashes.

"I've missed seeing you, Tom," Xanae said, and I felt so deeply for her wounded spirit while my hatred blazed anew for the dreadful Selena who brought this horror upon us.

We got through it, groups broke up and reformed while Selena licked her salacious lips with a vicious tongue. I knew for a certainty that if I could get our hostess alone on her balcony she would be tossed to her death with glee. But then Selena wasn't worth the killing; better she live her miserable existence to its bitter end.

Thereafter, I drank too much in steady gulps while mistress, Xanae and Selena avoided me. At some period in our dreadful evening a barracuda in black made sexual overtures in my direction. I suspect that she took note of the obvious and made a decision: if you want anything from that one you'd better get him in bed soon. As I continued to slop up booze I managed to convince the alcoholic mind that it was I who had been deceived and for this reason I decided to make a grand exit with the barracuda to prove my point. I had never seen her before and did not know her name. She was just there and a useful tool. As we left, I heard Selena scream, "Everyone is having an affair except me!"

I awoke the following day at noon, so an elegant clock read, once I could focus, and I would have willed my head to science without hesitation. Through a series of grimaces, gropings, moans and groans, I found the floor and managed to stand with aid from the four-poster of ancient vintage which had expensive antique written all over it. Early reactions gave me reason to feel that I was floating in air, as one sometimes feels when waking from sleep on a long flight. With some careful turning of the head I decided that I was on the rear of the house. Making my way to the door, I saw faint light in the foreground and deduced, if drunks can, that the front of the house might be in that direction. With all this mental activity caroming through my pained head, I staggered along the hallway, past two baths and into a second boudoir. Pushing aside the draperies, which affected me as would fingernails on glass, I looked out on a combination of fog and sun and saw Alcatraz straight ahead. Beyond the Island, San Francisco lay in all its grandeur while to the right of the City I could see a bit of the Golden Gate Bridge. I was in some person's house high on a hill in Sausalito. I was shocked, to say the least.

Vaguely, I remembered leaving Selena's bash with a woman in black who upon first sight I categorized as a barracuda. For the sake of clarity, I should explain that in the lexicon of the stud, a barracuda is a man-eating broad only one step less dangerous than a piranha. Perhaps the main difference between the two is that the piranha can strip the flesh from male bones a wee bit faster than her barracuda sister.

Taking note of my condition, I found that I was still dressed as of the night before, including shoes. I entered the first bathroom where I could wash my face and stare at the image of self-destruction that looked back at me. My mouth felt foul, a gargle of trusty Listerine helped. I checked my person for valuables, such as wallet and keys and found that all were in place. My confidence was raised a whit when I looked in my wallet and found an unbroken fifty and three stray one dollar bills. Obviously, it was beyond my capacity to walk down the curving hills of Sausalito to the town area so I decided that I should summon a taxi. Hand on phone, a light of recognition flashed within my head and I faced the fact that I didn't know the address. This made necessary my creeping descent from second to first floor. With front door opened, I winced from the brilliance of the day as I looked about for a street sign. A corner lot helped for ahead I made out the sign that read Cresta Verde and as I turned back to re-enter the house I took note of the number to the right of the door. Back inside, I called a cab and gave the vital statistics adding, I think, which brought a rude rejoinder from a vile-minded dispatcher.

The kitchen was on the first floor front and was a marvel of modern gadgetry, so I observed as I approached the frig for a beer. As I closed the box, beer in hand, I noticed the hand-scrawled note stuck to the refrigerator door which read: thanks for nothing.

"Ungrateful bitch," I muttered, as I sat down to sip much needed nourishment and to wait for a cab. "Bitches and bastards, too," I added, as I commenced to review Selena's party and her fiendish accomplishments. To hell with all of them, I told myself, as I resented all the vulgar commentaries on my behavior anrJ how I deserved to be caught with the evidence times three by a well-planned face-to-face between mistress and ballerina. As for the husbands of all these female wretches, who were licking their chops as well, over weight goons who were glad to have had me amuse their wives but who were suddenly filled with pseudo self-righteous indignation. At my expense the lot of them were able to save face. I tried to think, to prepare my defense, as I returned to San Francisco via a Greyhound bus.

4.

Fog was turning Russian Hill into an impressionist painting as the taxi dumped me at my mistress' flat. I entered and spoke, she made unidentifiable throat noises while flipping through the pages of a prominent fashion magazine.

Finally, she said, "Selena was quite clever with her sordid little coup. That's the only reason I accepted her invitation. It was a divine chance to let her cut her scrawny neck with a dull knife. Now there will be two of you to suffer together. I was rather sorry for the Ballerina but she'll learn from the experience. I'm packed for Paris and will be leaving tomorrow for the Spring showings. A bit early, of course, but who knows, I may meet a charming young Frenchman. I'll be gone for several months. You may stay in the flat while you get yourself together, if that is possible. Otherwise, let's keep our parting on a civil plain. When I return, I expect to find you gone."

My former mistress left the flat before dawn of the next day for her flight to Paris. I heard the cab door slam and knew that she was gone. My head hurt for several days as I crept about the flat with a monumental case of self-pity. The frig became bare and canned goods went in spectacular fashion. The worse I felt, the hungrier I became, or so it seemed. I tried to cash a check on our mutual bank account only to find that the account had been closed, so a fat clerk advised with great satisfaction. I admired my former mistress' efficiency if nothing else.

On a morning when the pain was seemingly unbearable I went to the loft where I modeled and where the Ballet worked out. Once more, I asked among her peers for knowledge of her whereabouts and none knew anything about her absence. One day, she just didn't show. A friend of hers was able to tell me that she had called Xanae's home number but the mother spoke only in Greek and no communication was possible.

Desperation breeds inspiration .. perhaps... for I suddenly remembered Silvio and his yellow cab and how I smelled the day of my fishing expedition. From the loft, I half-walked, half-ran downtown to Yellow Cab headquarters Gasping for breath, I explained to a bored dispatcher my tale of woe. "On Wednesday last, early afternoon, I hailed a taxi near the fishing fleet docks and he took me to my residence on Russian Hill. He'll remember me because I stank of fish. He may be Greek."

"Sounds like Silvio to me but he ain't Greek, he's Italian."

"His cab number was 632, I remember!"

The dispatcher shuffled papers and said, "Yeah, that was Silvio. You looking for a ride or a lay? Silvio will go with anybody."

"No, I am not trying to make out with Silvio and I don't need a cab. I think he knows some people, a girl. She's Greek and her brothers own a fishing boat. When can I talk with Silvio?"

More papers were shuffled before the old goat advised, "He's on a run to Candlestick Park."

"When will he be back, I wailed, "I'll pay for his time, in fact, he can take me to Russian Hill."

The mention of money aroused the dispatcher from his state of lethargy and via radio, he informed Silvio that he had a fare, "The one who smelled like fish." I heard Silvio cackle and announce that he'd be in shortly.

I ran toward Yellow 632 before Silvio could properly park as the monstrous dispatcher yelled, "Remember, Silvio will go with anybody." I gave the creep my stiff arm at the elbow.

Silvio grinned and said, "You smell better than last time."

"Thanks. Do you know the Greek brothers who own the fishing boat called the Xanae? It was named after their sister."

"Yeah, sure. The Xanae belongs to the Constontatos family. There are six brothers and we drink retsina at a Greek bar out in the Mission. They're a mean bunch, but if they like you, you've got friends for life."

"Well, they don't like me. I'm in love with their sister."

"Man, you've got a problem."

"She's dropped out of the Ballet and when I call the house I'm cursed in Greek and nobody will talk English with me."

"So you're the one," Silvio remarked, shaking his head. "They sent her to their Greek Island to come to her senses and the word is out. If that guy she's shacked up with...and that's you.. comes to the Island, there's a reward for anyone who puts a bullet between his eyes."

I slumped in my seat and sighed with resignation. "Do you know the name of the Island?" I asked.

"No. And for your sake, I'm glad I don't." Silvio squeezed my knee and I felt somewhat less of a lost soul. At the flat, as I paid and tipped, Silvio gave me his card. "Call any time, pal, if you get lonely."

Once inside the flat, I went to the nearest wall and beat my head against it as I cried, "She's gone, she's gone. They've taken her from me and I'll never see her again," I raged, banging my head against a wooden closet door as a change of scenery. "I must kill her," I screamed, "I must learn to believe that she is dead. I must believe. I must kill in order to live without her."

Slowly, but inevitably, it became obvious to my bruised head that I had to find employment were I to meet those necessary requirements otherwise known as food, clothing and shelter were I to have a future with some degree of solvency, the latter seemingly unlikely to a distraught lover who lost mistress and lover at the same time. I reached a subterranean depth where I even thought of visiting Selena, the viper in my bosom, so that I might throw her off her balcony for ruining my life. None should care, in her case, except the fuzz, who would arrest me for Murder One instead of Justifiable Homicide. There should be an open season on vermin like Selena. I never could understand why her husband could put up with her. Perhaps that is why he traveled a lot.

I thought of the barracuda who took me to Sausalito for nought but I didn't know her name or phone number and even if I did I had doubts as to the status of my welcome. All of my avenues to living on charm seemed to be closing around me. I felt a kinship with all those wealthy souls who threw themselves from high-rise windows as the banks closed in 1929. I had become an unmarketable toy, a snake, a stale and worn stud who should be in his prime, a pariah, an untouchable. I began to feel like a prisoner in San Francisco, a state of mind that defies logic in one of the most free spots on earth. Becoming a bit hysterical, I saw myself as a convict about to order his last meal while the

31

thought of employment assumed ominous proportions. But when one is young and dumb, something always turns up.

A friend called and asked me out for drinks at a Polk Street bar, an invitation that I grabbed with greedy hands. Over a frosty pitcher of margaritas, he told me that he had joined the American Red Cross as an Assistant Field Director in their Service to Military Installations program. All this was gibberish to my ears as all I knew about the Red Cross was that they collected blood. After listening to my sad tale of betrayal and desertion friend suggested that I seek similar employment.

"They'll hire anybody," he declared, "What have you got to lose." he quipped, hitting a raw nerve. "Foreign service is inevitable; a change of scenery will do you good."

I followed my addlepated friend's advice and was hired as he predicted. I entered the same training class as he and we were shipped to a dismal military installation near Sacramento for training. There I met an old timer in the ARC by name of Sybil who hung a hip on my door and drawled, "Mah specialty is death messages, what's yours?" Sybil helped keep me alive and relatively sane during that trying time with her putdowns, biting humor and caustic wit while I broke out with a case of neurodermatitis, while I developed an inner ear infection, all of it symptomatic of what is euphemistically referred to as a nervous breakdown. It took six months to recover and I say, bless you, Syb, old girl, wherever you may be.

I spent a year and a half floating from military installation to military installation, all of them in California which I recall as a round-robin of boredom. If ever spinning one's wheels applied, it applied to me, for I knew that I should be at Cal finishing my Doctorate. But I wasn't and so the day came when orders were cut for my assignment to Korea. In Tokyo, the fleshpots lured and then I met Fran, another old Red Cross regular, an international gypsy as all of us become who follow the foreign service route. Fran was assigned to the Navy Hospital in Yokusaka, which is a posh spot, a garden of Eden that begins the Japanese Riviera. Before I departed for Korea, Fran decided that she was in love with me. Wealthy, from a first marriage, I coined the neat phrase that successful lawyers make wealthy widows but Fran was not amused.

Her sudden passion for me did not impose any financial problems as she owned a condo on Chicago's North Shore where she could keep me handsomely. The problem was the age difference as I was almost young enough to be her son. To her everlasting credit, I must salute her for her mid-western common sense that kept her from becoming involved with a guy who would forever be referred to as her young lover.

My stay in Korea was brief. I loathed social work and the pretense that the Red Cross had some valid reason for being there was spurious as any chaplain or first sergeant could perform the same functions. In truth, the Red Cross disliked me as strongly as I disdained them as I did not treat their services as some missionary calling. And so I quit, which in their clerical modus operandi meant that I had become persona non grata as I had failed to fulfill my contract. They were duty bound to return me to the States and the point of my hiring but flights were not available to one so discredited as myself. I would be returned home via military ship, better known as the diaper run, a vessel filled with screaming military brats and horny mothers. The term send me home was too patently paternalistic for me to swallow so I informed the ARC that I would return to San Francisco as I damned well pleased.

Before departure, however, I decided that I would tour Japan which would be a relief from bars and officers' clubs. Having already severed ARC connections, I became a tourist in earnest making firstly the journey to Sapporo, the capital city of Hokaido. As it turned out, I loved this far northern city and left with sadness. Back in Tokyo for a few days of rest and then I took the train to Osaka and the southernmost Island of Kyushu. I made a point of traveling to the tip of the southern island where I removed my shoes and walked on miles of tropical beach.

I returned to Tokyo seething with a desire to get back to the States for I had reached the conclusion that I wasn't cut out to live the life of an expatriate, but before I could book passage I received correspondence from Absalom Prevet's lawyer advising me that Absalom had died and that the house on Potrero Hill belonged to me exclusively, having been placed in joint tenancy several years earlier. The Doctor was constantly threatening to do it and I would say no, but one day, he shoved some forms at me and said <u>sign</u> and I did, lost in my right brain and with no cognizance of the significance of my signature. I wondered if he sent me via telepathy notice of his demise and that it was time to come home and get my ass back in Cal there to finish my doctoral thesis.

As much as I loved Absalom, which I could never call him, his incessant chatter was seldom taken seriously which it should have been, for in his peculiar manner, Prevet was a master of duplicity. Look at my life if you have any doubts.

Now that I owned the rustic cottage made of fine wood, with a downtown and East Bay view, it dawned upon me that I also owned Cain and Abel and the cats, Ying and Yang, now in the care of Mama Cabrini, our next-door neighbor now keeper of the beasties until the day of my return. At which time, I would assume my parental duties, a thought that shattered. Strangely, as long as the pets belonged to the Professor, I adored them. Now I felt trapped. Having never experienced a traditional home environment, I threw myself on my bed and wept for all the orphans of the storm. Storm abated, I booked passage on a modern combination freighter and passenger vessel filled with cargo that was San Francisco bound. The crew was entirely Japanese and so was the cuisine. Fortunately₁ I love Japanese food while an English couple aboard blanched each time they approached the ship's mess. I also developed a spinal problem from the incessant bowing and the uttering of a thousand <u>dozos</u> each day but an ample supply of sake helped me float across the azure Pacific in more ways than one.

I wanted to grieve for Absalom on this quixotic journey but I knew that he wouldn't approve so I tried to recall all the hysterical escapades we had shared beginning with the day that I dropped my pants in Berkeley and became his prize model.

My final affair in Southern California lasted longer than intended but then affairs are devilishly difficult to predict. Cal Tech has better luck soothe saying earthquakes but once settled in Berkeley I felt the stirring of new beginnings and the letting go of a painful past. I settled in a tiny room in the Doctor's school residence, as he called it, and the Doctor saw that I had all the modeling work I could handle and when modeling was slow he became quite adept at playing pimp when the need arose. None has never complimented me on my brains, except my-self, for without the brains I could not have sustained a ninety-two average with my modeling and assignation assignments. I felt offended, once or twice.

"Thank God, you're young and healthy and with an infinite capacity for orgasms," the Doc was to reiterate often, "And should you die of penis exhaustion, I'll make sure that you're buried with proper ceremony. The chaps at the lab will enjoy the task. What a marvelous epitaph it shall be: here lies an eternal erection, may it rest in piece."

Doc retired while my thesis remained a wad of notes and scribbled ideas. He insisted that I return to Potrero Hill to be with the animals and himself but, stubbornly, I chose to remain in his wee Berkeley cottage. "Once the thesis is finished, I shall return to San Francisco. It is a promise." To which the Professor muttered to the pets that all of us should live so long. Abel raised his right paw in understanding.

"It's the perfect place to hide from tricks, mistresses and other pests." Sighed the annoyed Professor, "Your greatest weakness, dear boy, is the dissipation of your bodily fluids."

I'd spent so much time there that establishing residence was somewhat redundant, and yet I demurred. The dear Doctor had an infinite capacity for taking over one's existence and I feared that being under thumb, as it were, he'd turn me into a withered old satyr by the time I was forty what with daily modeling classes, nightly assignations and a thesis that wouldn't write itself. In truth, the Doctor's schedule was beginning to take the pleasure out of my work. Brilliant artist and teacher he was; I often think that he missed his calling and should have run a house of nubile boys. Such an endeavor would have gone well with his penchant for Dickensean prose. Then one could say that the Doctor had a sufficient menagerie without me. What with Cain and Abel, two dashing Dobermans who looked ferocious but were lovers at the core. Then there was Ying and Yang, two of the meanest Siamese I have ever met, who would remove your eyes in a second. Ying and Yang dominated Cain and Abel completely and the Doctor as well.

Vividly, do I recall my first visit to his house in San Francisco. The Professor appeared in the back yard with whip in hand, wearing jodphurs, a red satin shirt and a vest of flamboyant plaid while a billowing black cape was tied about his neck. A jaunty top hat completed his ensemble. He reminded me most of a friendly Dracula as at a command in one of his many languages the cats jumped upon the backs of the dogs and around the yard they sped. Those sharp claws imbedded in the hides of Cain and Abel made me cringe until I came to realize that all four were delirious with joy while performing their circus caper. The louder the cats purred, the happier they were.

To the north of the Doctor's cottage lived Mama Cabrini, a roly-poly Italian sweetheart who preferred to live alone rather than with any of her large brood. The Professor and his pets were much more exciting than sniveling grandchildren. Then there was juicy gossip to tell her priest during confessions. Hearing about happenings at the Professor's casita caused Franciscan hairs to rise. I was added to her list as just another lost soul who needed loving care and good Italian food.

On the south side of the Doc's house lived Boris and Mathilde. Boris had been tortured by the Nazis during the War and his legs were badly damaged. Knowing dear Mathilde, as I do, I have found it difficult to reconcile her gentle nature and her gourmet cuisine with having been a member of the French Resistance who saved Boris and other Russian captives from the Germans. To Mathilde went the honor of her peers as she was selected for the slitting of the German Captain's throat. I have no doubt but what she gave to the doomed Officer the same detached perfection that she gives to the removal of a gander's head.

Boris' legs might be of little use but there was genius in his shoulders, arms and hands for sculpture and in his sixties he was becoming famous. Mathilde smiled softly as she worshiped Boris, the Professor, the cats and dogs and would continue to make magnificent soufflés and ratatouilles for the lot of us. For the animals, she made beef liver pate which they slurped with gusto. So one can perceive that my reluctance to move in had something to do with adolescent pride about keeping a few secret hours for myself plus a fear of commitment that has haunted me for most of my life.

I talked to the spirit of the Professor a great deal on our steady passage from Yokohama to Oakland. I held nothing back. On the bow of the boat, alone with thoughts and salt spray, it was so easy to hold nothing back, to let go with it.

Not many ships enter the Golden Gate in brilliant sun and we were no exception. We picked up the fog near the Farralones and slithered our way through the Golden Gate and under the Bay Bridge to our berth along the Oakland pier. Mario, he of the Italian Thunderclap, was there to greet me. We hugged a lot and guzzled beer while I was clearing customs. When Mario's wagon was loaded with my meagre possessions we made our way across the Bay Bridge and leftward toward Potrero Hill. At the Doctor's house, now my house, Mario placed my gear on the front stoop and said, "Don't ask me to come in. Mama Cabrini will insist on an Italian reunion and I have had all of those I can bear. Call for lunch after you recover."

Fog hovered in the valleys but on the crest of Potrero Hill the sun shone brilliantly as I raised the metal latch to the rear gate and tried to make an unobtrusive entrance into the back yard.

Later, Mama Cabrini was to tell me, "They knew the day and the hour you left Japan and they have been waiting and fussing and blaming Boris, Mathilde and me about the time it was taking for you to get home."

Said Mathilde: "Boris built gates between our three yards so that they could visit."

"Of recent days," Boris explained, they just lay on the rear deck and waited. Finally, they quit eating so we brought pate and force-fed them."

When they got to me, I fell on the ground in self-defense while two angry dogs and two vicious cats had their way with me. I was licked, bitten, scratched, barked at and scolded. Finally, they let me stand so that I could embrace Mama Cabrini,

Mathilde and Boris, mess that I was. After a shower and change of clothes Mathilde fed us coq au vin while the dogs slept on my feet and the cats purred their satisfaction.

Several days later, Mama Cabrini interrupted my onerous task of unpacking and searching for I knew nothing about Absalom's private files. The public person, I knew well; the private one played games with me, games that I never won. Mama Cabrini was fingering her rosary which meant that she had serious thoughts to impart and that I was not to ignore the Savior's decisions which were usually hers via earthly intervention. She sat on the worn couch in Absalom's tiny living room with two Siamese cats making a fur about her fat little neck, all of it a bit campy but endearing, as she stated her case. "Tomasino, we must take them to the cemetery so that they will know where the Doctor lies. Once they know, they will accept his passing. Will you take us there?"

"Of course, Mama," I declared, as I wiped sweat and book dust from my brow. "Where is he buried?"

"In Colma " she explained.

"In Colma," I yelled, startling the cats. "That's Cemetery City!" referring to the small town just south of San Francisco which has more graveyards per capita than most of surburbia has tracts.

On a day selected by Mama Cabrini, we curried the animals and locked them in the Doctor's old wagon then set our sights southward to Colma where people sometimes fall into a state of morbidity and conjecture on the source of meat in their burgers.

"The animals are excited," I said, observing their prancing and mewling, "They know where we are going."

"Of course, my darling, animals are strongly clairvoyant. What a pity we lost ours."

"We didn't lose it, Mama, it lies dormant within us."

"As a Catholic, I am not supposed to believe. But I do."

"Bless you, Mama."

We drove through several cemeteries, one blending into another, each recognizable by religious symbols, most of them bearing far-out names such as Angels' Wings or Glorious Rest and finally, I looked at a Star of David as Mama announced, "Here, dear, take the next right turn. I will direct you."

I followed Mama's instructions until we were traversing a final resting place filled with Stars of David. "Mama," I asked slow on the upbeat, "We're in a Jewish Cemetery." Mama crossed herself several times but did not answer, which led me to ask:

"Was Absalom Jewish?"

"Oh, yes," she exclaimed, weeping into her scented handkerchief.

"Believe it or not, I never knew. And the thought never occurred and if it had, it would have been of little significance to me. I am indifferent to such things while Absalom was truly a man of all seasons defying category."

"Neither did I," Mama wept. "I would have married him but my children would have disowned me. The plot is to the right, dear boy," she added, sensing my uncertainty.

Mama wiped her tiny red nose as we parked along the narrow road between blocks of neat plots filled with Stars of David. As we released the animals we took note of their serious mein and as I walked forward I realized that we were facing a double plot which seemed to be our destination.

The one on the left drew my attention. I ran my palms across the polished granite on which was recorded Absalom Prevet, Professor Emeritus, born February 4, and remembered with a shock that he and I shared the same birthday. "Fellow Aquarians have much to ponder," I recalled. "Absalom didn't believe in death." I explained to Mama. "He detested the alleged finiteness of it. Birthdays were acceptable for they signified that one was still in the flesh and could do it all over again."

With unaccustomed dignity, the dogs walked forward on either side of me and as we reached the headstone they rose on their rear paws so that they might sniff the top and sides of the stone while the cats walked around the rough material scratching their backs and purring loudly. At which time, I muttered to the monument as though the stone could hear, "You are an impossible old fraud."

Cain and Abel claimed their territory with spurts of urine on both sides of the stone. Discreetly, the cats followed their routine in a most elegant manner. In their way, I was convinced that they knew this was the other home where Absalom went when he was not at the house on Potrero Hill.

Nama Cabrini came forward and placed a single rose on the monument as she said to the animals, "This is a token of love for our dear Professor. While he sleeps here, he is always with us." The cats whined while Cain and Abel went to the left corners of the plot to further mark their territory.

Overcome by so much, I was slow to become cognizant of a second headstone on the right side of the plot. Even as I saw, my eyes refused to believe so I looked at Mama, a question mark on my face, as I said, "It's for me. It has my name on it." Nothing else but my name and date of birth, February 4, but once again, no year was given. Below it, I read my epitaph which Absalom had not forgotten. It read: rest in piece, eternal erection.

As I waited for Mama to speak, the dogs and cats squirted urine on the right corners of the plot meant for me. "Mama, I'm not Jewish, not in this life. And I've willed my remains to the University Hospital." At which time, I stretched out on the grass the length of my unchosen plot and talking aloud, I decided, "I'll give my organs for harvest and let the rest of me be buried here." At which time, Cain and Abel squirted my clean jeans with urine thus sealing our pact. Reflecting upon these sudden changes in destiny, I muttered, "Thank God, I've been circumcised." Mama Cabrini crossed herself in a Jewish Cemetery and wept into her handkerchief. Satisfied, the animals made their way to Absalom's old wagon and waited patiently for me to open the rear door so that they could enter for our trip to the other home.

5.

Once settled in I set about my voyage of discovery which led me to understand that Absalom never threw anything away. Three desks were crammed with notebooks and memorabilia. Partial manuscripts, photographs and legal documents that I found incomprehensible were part of the larder. Candy hardened in its wrapper must have been fresh during World War I. Keys were everywhere but it took days before I discovered the one which unlocked the third desk as yet untouched by my plundering hands.

At night, I would wake up to find Cain and Abel, Ying and Yang sitting in a row and illuminated by the streetlight that shone through the front bedroom window. I knew that they were visiting with the spirit of Absalom and when in the company of those he loves, Abel has a habit of lifting his right front paw and putting it down with emphasis as though he agreed with what was being said. I felt Absalom's presence during the days, also, as if he were filled with glee to watch me make an effort to clean up his junk and especially my frustration with the third desk.

One night I dreamed that I was back in the art class as naked as the day of my birth while Absalom berated me for being so obtuse and I seemed to hear him say: it's in the third desk, you fool. Search, search! Or do you want it all given to you on the proverbial silver platter.

He visited Mama Cabrini, Mathilde and Boris, too, and they never failed to apprise me. I think that we came to expect visitations from Absalom for as long as we were alive or lived in or near his house. Eventually, his visits became commonplace. If Mathilde couldn't find some object sorely needed, she would reach the conclusion that Absalom had hidden it from her, the tease, as she was wont to call him.

I am not one to hoard grudges or to hold onto pain or to savor one-upmanship. No bouquets, please! It has been said by rejected lovers that I am too shallow to care while others blame my indifference on a high I. Q. What they mean but can't articulate properly is that Thomas Richard Stone does not tolerate yokes about his neck, although I now wear a chain bearing the Star of David in honor of Absalom even while I curse him for the riddle to the third desk. Once, I became so pissed that I thought seriously of renting an electric saw and reducing the desk to pieces yet there was potential danger in such behavior as whatever rested within might no longer be there after the sawdust caper. Gertrude Stein was right, I informed Ying, who hissed at me, after the saw there might not be any there there, to paraphrase her famous remark about her unloved home town of Oakland.

Further and more personal, Mama Cabrini would never forgive me for such a desecration for to her the antique walnut desk was an extension to her Catholic alter. The thought of Absalom sitting at his walnut desk among her Catholic saints reduced me to uncontrollable laughter.

Upon my return from the Orient I sent the house key to my former mistress' office, return receipt requested. At our first luncheon, following my return, Mario informed me that a Mexican drag queen had absconded to a life of luxury on Selena's prized jewelry. Generously, he offered to buy Selena airline tickets should she like to visit him in Cuernavaca. I, in turn, informed Mario that press clippings of Xanae's wedding were sent to me anonymously, in Selena' s spidery script, while I was in Korea. I found it sweet to hear that Selena's jewel box had been rifled by a greedy little hairburner. Her come-uppance was long overdue.

Several lunches later, Mario took me to a new spot which had opened while I was in the Orient. It turned out to be a tasteless pickup joint serving dreadful food and was built as a double carousel with one circle of seats moving clockwise while the other moved in a counter clockwise direction thus making it impossible not to see or be seen as one perused the wares. Prices were ridiculous but Mario who is a social gadfly adored the place as he is forever in search of any member of any gender whom he can mount. For good reason, I blame this disaster on him for if I were for hire, I would demand combat pay before entering such a dive.

We caught up quickly, referring to what had transpired while I was abroad. We became intoxicated and cried Viva! this and Viva! that. Viva senioritis, viva borrachos, viva putas and mariposas, which pretty well took care of those congregated therein. We became sufficiently drunk to think that we were clever when in reality we were drunken bores in an expensive pickup joint. Joy of joys, my former mistress was there with a coven of anorexic models representing three or four different genders. Vaguely, former mistress smiled at me and wiggled her pinkie. I, in turn, gave her the Churchillian two-digit sign of victory with the stiffest fingers I could make. Observing her motley group, I muttered, "Fruits and nuts," a bit too loudly.

To which Mario replied, "I'll give them my Italian sausage for adequate compensation."

By this time, the starchy maitre d' approached our spot and slapped a bill on our table as he declared, "Pay and depart. We don't cater to riffraff and we suggest that you never come again."

"I'll give you my Italian sausage for a hundred bucks," Mario declared. At which time, the maitre d' snapped his fingers and brought forth two beefy bouncers who took us under arms and threw us out of this pseudo elegant bistro which traded in live flesh and bad cuisine. A new career buds for me as I am now persona non grata in one of the newer pickup places.

As we came to a bit and scrambled to our feet, I brushed dust from my clothes and whistled for a cab in which I shoveled Mario into the back seat. Fortunately, I was able to find my vehicle where I had left it. Once home, I slept for a long while as the dogs and cats kept their distance as they dislike the smell of drunks. Eventually, the fumes evaporated and I sobered sufficiently for the animals to find me socially acceptable again and it was at this juncture that I approached desk number three and gave it a kick with the toe of my Reebock which produced unexpected results. There was a metallic thud and tinkle as some inner part fell from place one to place two. In a frenzy, I tried and opened doors and drawers heretofore forbidden to me and in the process of opening and closing, I failed to take note that Yang was perusing one of the drawers, and as I closed the door I caught the end of his tail. Such howls of outrage you can only imagine and as I opened the drawers, and Yang sprang free leaving me with a bloody finger. Once free, he flew to the top of the mantle there to howl, hiss and give vent to his wounded pride for the rapidly swishing tail was evidence a plenty that damage was minimal. I apologized profusely as the tail went faster and throaty moans told me precisely what Yang thought of me for the moment. How quickly do we become slaves to beasties of the alleged lower order. Lower, hell! They're a million times more intelligent than their human counterparts so I have begun to learn.

What I found in the bowels of the walnut desk was a manuscript box filled with professionally typed pages. As I thumbed through, from back to front, I saw quotes from my unfinished thesis which made me feel creepy for I was beholding a finished product which I had barely begun. As this occurred, I began to feel that I had been left behind in time and as I paused to study phrases and paragraphs done so well that I longed to have written them myself while knowing that I had not and if not then who and why. With these thoughts burgeoning through my brain, I turned back to the beginning and found the letter from Absalom to me.

Dear Favorite Model: Copyright on your thesis has already been applied for under your name and should arrive soon. Keep a copy in a safe place until the copyright has been received. Pity I didn't take care of that before I left but one cannot think of everything when time is running out. Although I am definitely responsible for your inability to finish your thesis, I have no guilt whatsoever. There was so much for you to learn, so many flowers to be picked, so many lovelies to be mounted and having had it all, I wanted you to savor the last drop of nectar from the source as I had done, to know joie de vivre in every conceivable way, and so I have played games with you again.

I saw in your notes and drafts a certain lack of style. Your work lacked pizzazz. While it is true that you are the better writer, I have the sauce, the zest that makes the better sound. Thus, dear boy, I can now admit what you have already discerned: I am an adorable fraud, a precious thief who doesn't steal money, he steals bits and pieces of people he admires. Yet in my own peculiar way, I do believe that I have managed to repay to each of you from whom I have taken a bit more than I swiped. Shameless me! I offer no apologies.

And so! Whilst you were spreading your viable ass about the Orient, I wrote the thesis for you. No groveling thanks, please, it wouldn't become you. Furthermore, I did it with vengeance aforehand. The alleged Professor of English Lit, Gustav Hauptman, whom you know well, is a twit, and it is he who will pass on your work without having read one bloody page of it. This charlatan will pass it on to one of his favorite boys who will do the reading for him and you will be given a B. Have you never wondered why none ever gets an A! I wanted to make damned sure that Hauptman's boys were so titillated that they would give you an A without second thought. And they shall.

In this, our golden age of camp, you shall get an A. Of course, you may scream at what I've done but my mission will be accomplished by changing the title.. and listen carefully... to THE EFFECT OF HOMOSEXUALITY ON LITERATURE FROM PLATO TO TENNESSEE WILLIAMS. Pick yourself off the floor, dear boy, and learn to love it. You will be famous for a lifetime which beats Warhol and his fifteen minutes. It's simply too campy not to click.

Make copies for yourself and then mail the thesis and letter to Hauptman in the enclosed manuscript box. I wager that you'll hear from him in record time.

It was so much fun knowing you and remolding you from the bourgeoisie you tried to be. Pardom me for gloating but I feel that I did a brilliant piece of work. I knew you had the potential the first time you dropped your pants.

Stunned, I sat on the floor, until my legs grew numb, until Yang grew curious and returned to the desk once again to sniff Absalom's presence in the papers surrounding me. Undone, I grabbed Yang and kissed him. Which so shocked him that he fled to the kitchen and wouldn't even come out for dinner.

Absalom was right, of course. I could write the same thesis but it would lack the pizzazz, the flow, the shimmer. As for the contents, many of his thoughts and ideas I would never have thought about for there is still that part of me that can only go mad in a reserved sort of way while Absalom was happy in a state of utter and complete insanity and loved every moment of it.

I complied with Absalom' s instructions, to the letter, and he was right. In less than a month, Hauptman called to congratulate me on a brilliant piece of work which was doomed to be published. And would I have lunch soon, so that he could go through the charade of an oral examination. Clearly, he had read the script as he made verbatum quotes from time to time. During our chat, the dogs and cats cavorted about the room and I knew that they were celebrating with the spirit of Absalom.

At our luncheon, Hauptman made his announcement. "SFSU wants you to teach Creative Writing full time. Stanford has nibbled, likewise UCLA and Northwestern. It's the thesis, isn't it."

"Indubitably! I never knew that I was so talented."

"Neither did I," Hauptman confessed.

"I'll do two days of teaching at SFSU as I don't want to leave San Francisco. That will give me time for personal creativity. With the publication of the thesis I shall have crossed the rubicon: I need no longer publish or perish in the Groves of Academe. I write because I must. Those who can.. ..... do"

Wringing his hands with ecstasy, Hauptman completed my remark by adding: "While those who can't.. .teach. God help us if we misquoted the old bastard. Right now, Thomas, the system will agree to anything in order to get you on campus. Really, I had no idea that you could be so witty."

"One grows," I announced, with a shrug.

SFSU herniated themselves in their efforts to secure the academic catch of the season.. .Doctor Thomas Richard Stone... who had been called many things on that loose campus of higher learning. I made it easy for them; they did what I wanted; contracts were signed for two Creative Writing classes a week and there was a clause giving me freedom to model in my spare time, with or without clothing. The signing of contracts demanded the presence of my long-time agent, Cyrus Benatar, who flew up from Los Angeles for the momentous occasion.

46

When Cyrus finally got it through his smog-filled noggin that Doctor Thomas Richard Stone was calling the cards, this unbelievable state of affairs gave poor Cy a mini-heart attack but he recovered quickly as agents do and accepted my new status as Doctor of Literature with thesis soon to be published and took an overly generous share of the credit which belonged and rightly so to my late mentor, Absalom Prevet.

Everlastingly an agent to the core, Cyrus began to hustle. "You're not gonna teach until mid-September and here it is not yet the end of June. Now there's a crazy Arab pushing a new line of mens swim wear and they want you to represent them. Big bucks and no brains, the perfect set-up. My God, Sweet Cakes, how do you manage to look only twenty years younger than I with the life you've led. If I didn't know better, I'd think that Absalom Prevet was coaching you on the side."

"Absalom was my mentor, of course he's coaching me on the side, as you put it. But purity of heart has a lot to do with my success. In my heart, I am as pure as manufactured snow. Now what do the filthy rich Arabs want me to do?"

"They're doing a new line of chic men's' swim wear which they stole from Brazil and Argentina. Only theirs are for men only as Arab broads are never seen except for their eyes. It's a G-string outfit with a miniature pouch to hold your bat and balls and they show all you've got. Some come with sequins, some with precious stones. Who knows, they may do you in a fig leaf but who cares. The money is good and all you've got to do is spread your ass around the globe but what else is new, you've been doing that for years."

"When will this photographic session occur, how long will it take and can I get back to school on time?"

"They want to photograph in Puerta Vallarta as soon as possible and they're set up for a four-day shoot. You'll be back in time for first class."

"I loathe Puerta Vallarta; it's a Mexican Disneyland. What is the fee?"

Cy was reluctant to say for fear I'd queer the deal, not yet acquainted with the new me. "One hundred thou and one percent royalties worldwide."

Even I was impressed. "Where do I sign?"

After another mini-heart attack, Cy called the camel drivers in Los Angeles and confirmed a deal. Boris, Mathilde and Mama Cabrini agreed to care for the pets, as I knew they would. "I am so fortunate to have such loving friends." I cried, kissing everyone. When I was packed and ready to depart, I told the pets that I had to be gone for a few days. The cats hissed while the dogs licked my face and made me weep.

I assumed that we would meet the Arabs in a posh hotel and grew bewildered when we were whisked from LAX to Bel Air in a rented limo. The estate from which the Arabs operated was a mini-version of the Shangri-La with overtones of Hollywood bad taste. There were two of them, one a fat little man very much the motherly type while his associate was tall, lean, arrogant and spoke excellent English. Such swishing of white robes would make a drag queen lose her confidence. Running hither and yon I saw females with covered faces and a series of male caretakers to attend to one's slightest need. The mansion floated in incense which drove my allergies crazy. Contracts were signed and we agreed to depart for Puerta Vallarta the following afternoon with favorable weather reports. The fat little Arab smiled at me with adoring eyes until the arrogant one told him to behave himself, I assume, as the little one became less obvious in his amorous pursuits. As soon as Cy and I were alone, I growled, "You'd better make these crazy people pay in cash and try to remember, my body is not part of the deal except in front of a camera."

I am not in love with Puerta Vallarta and the day of our arrival did nothing to change my point of view. The weather had turned sullen, still and uneasy from threatening hurricanes. The set for our shoot was primitive, consisting of a small platform tethered to a group of trees growing out of the lagoon. On a second platform there was an electric motor which sucked water from the bay and sprayed it upon me to simulate my being drenched from hurricane forces. My hands were tied to a tree with leather thongs which was torture in short order while the blasts of water made the silly G-string itch fore and aft. The frontal portion of the alleged swim suit, a modern day version of the Elizabethan codpiece, wouldn't hide hairs on a flea's testicles, so there I was embracing a tree while water spewed upon me with manufactured ferocity. After three hours of this photographic torture I had been shot from every conceivable angle with everything that I own showing through the porous material from which shoulder pads and lapels are made, all of these indignities igniting a fire in my belly, as it were. Working free of my tether, I stepped away from the trees, ripped off my skimpy apparel and waded ashore as in a blind fury I walked toward our hotel. With cameras galore, las turistas took advantage of this golden opportunity while la policia showed many teeth as they tipped sombreros and adjusted their manhood in the tradition of machismo, a salute to my daring, as la senora with niño in hand clasped one voluminous breast with her free appendage and gasped, "Madre de Dios!" while covering the eyes of el niño with the other.

When I reached the lobby, staff on duty grabbed a tablecloth and rushed forward to envelope my nudity. On the elevator ride to my suite, several aroused males took advantage of my perilous state and copped a few feels of my anatomy. I was too spent to care.

For once, Cy had shown some prescience of mind and had cashed the Arabs' check before departure, which meant that we had made a hundred thou even if we never saw a sou of commissions from world-wide sales.

After some rest and a decent meal, my disposition improved and when I was confronted by the little Arab who reminds me of a nun, I made an effort to be gracious as he wrung his hands with numerous rings and cried, "Pleez, you must come and join my harem I weel geef you gold and silver, anything that your precious heart desires.

"I thought that harems were segregated," I retorted.

"Alas, they are. My country has peculiar rules of behavior."

"Sorry, chum, but I could not possible join a segregated harem. That would be against my religious principles."

"Theen I weel build you a personal harem with bathroom fixtures of gold while the bidet shimmers with precious stones, and eet weel be feeled with beautiful young boys, not one over the age of sixteen."

Thinking it over for a moment, I said, "What in the hell would I do with a bidet? In California, under aged boys are known as San Quentin quail or, if you prefer, segregation in reverse. Now please don't cry. " I entreated. Searching for excuses, I declared, "I'm under contract to the University of California for the next two years. After that, who knows!"

The little nun type put a handkerchief to his nose and wept his way from my suite. As much as I care for good old Cy, I began to think seriously that perhaps I had outgrown him.

The Arab bathing apparel was to be marketed under the name of Zozzy which I could only compare to a laxative. As I prepared for school during the dwindling days of summer, I almost forgot about our bizarre excursion to Puerta Vallarta and felt lucky to have been paid by such a nefarious undertaking, part of said funds going toward the purchase of a van for Boris and Mathilde, one of those especially equipped for the handicapped. Boris was preparing for his first show and the vehicle was sorely needed. I took much pleasure from being able to do for those I love, those who have done so much for me, a bona fide member of the walking wounded.

Once delivery had been made, all of us... Mama Cabrini, Boris and Mathilde, the dogs and cats and myself, .went for a ride with Boris driving. Mama Cabrini insisted that we stop for frozen yogurts for all.. people and animals.. and it became my chore to hold the cones for the cats while they licked their deserts and while mine melted. Their modus operandi for refreshments was to sink one cat claw into the cone and the other claw into the under side of my wrists. Heavy breathing on my part brought about a further digging of cat claws into my delicate flesh. By the time this ordeal was over melted yogurt mixed with blood covered my arms, wrist to elbow. I tossed the cats into the van and found a hydrant where I could wash away most of the evidence. For a spell of sublime brevity, I dreamed of exquisite techniques for doing away with two vicious felines.

As we prepared for the autumn semester, staff and students began to look forward to the first publicity on Zozzy's swim wear and on what must have been a dull news day the Chronicle broke the story out of all proportions to its news worthiness. I told all who asked, and truthfully, that I did not know the date that publicity would break or in what form it would appear. As events would transpire, anything that I might have said turned out to be an evasion or a lie for on Saturday prior to Monday classes anyone who had ever known me seemed to call and advise that Zozzy's billboard sat along the freeway going south. On the noon television news I was shocked afresh to see live films of policemen on foot hurrying traffic along. I saw it on my way to Monday classes and there I was tied to trees with rain pelting while the rag I wore was more provocative than full frontal nudity. For a brief moment, I wished that I was back in Ms. Reaves art class modeling for bored students, but those days were gone forever.

6.

I suspect that I approached my first day of teaching with the same indifference that I gave to Ms. Reaves' art classes which amounted to detachment and removal from a sense of reality. The giant Zozzy billboard sitting along the freeway ramp was a photograph and therefore unreal, or so I saw it. My naivete about the power of the media left me unprepared for what was to transpire.

I arrived at SFSU in time for breakfast at the cafeteria. I parked in the faculty lot in my newly captioned spot which read T. R. Stone. Briefcase in hand, I entered the Student Union to find a copy of the Zozzy ad stretching across one wall of the building. Scrawled across the white section were the words Welcome, Stud and before I could sit down with my coffee and cruller the crowded cafeteria burst into a simultaneous explosion: spoons beat on tables, knives and forks were played as musical instruments, whistles and catcalls were part of the cacophony. Finally, I saw the necessity of rising and waving to the crowd in hopes of bringing silence but to no avail. The madness continued until I left cruller and coffee untouched and fled from the building. Outside, on that foggy morning, I was hoisted on the shoulders of strong young men who carried me across the commons toward my classroom on the street side of the campus. When in Rome, speak Italian, I told myself, as I entered into the spirit of the occasion by waving my arms at the crowd all the while wondering why half the campus was serenading me.

My classroom turned out to be an auditorium suitable for those dull lecture courses for which students buy cribbed notes in order to avoid. As I was deposited behind the lectern on stage, I stood in awe as the auditorium filled to capacity. Even standing room became a premium. Half of those on campus wanted to take creative writing, so it appeared, while it was safe to surmise that half of that half were functional illiterates. I pulled the microphone into position and as they simmered down to a murmur, I heard myself say: "The man in the Zozzy ad is a myth." Incongruously, my words brought a roar of approval and

I had no idea why. Speaking from impulse, I heard myself say: "Don't become a writer if you can possibly avoid it." Once more, they roared approval which was beyond my comprehension. "Writing is an unhealthy occupation. It cramps your spine, enlarges your prostate or flattens your tush. Writing ruins your bowels and brings on leg cramps to the best of us. Writers are subject to hyper-tension, skin problems and sexual dysfunction. Writers keep psychiatrists in the upper income bracket. It takes guts supreme to stick a sheet of paper in a typewriter and the same guts to turn on your word processor. It takes ego supreme to feel that the world gives a damn about what you have to say. Writing is not an easy ticket to emotional and sexual fulfillment. Writing has more in common with lonely masturbation as you stare at a blank wall."

Warming to my subject, I continued. "But I don't think that you're here to celebrate the naked model in the Zozzy ad, I hope you're here to celebrate the stud who broke all the rules and lived to talk about it."

This declaration brought them to their feet and a full roar intermingled with catcalls and whistles. Obviously, I had struck a responsive chord. When they were once more quiet, I carried on. 'Only thirty students will take this course per semester for creative writing occurs in quiet places and not at a political rally. For your assignment next week, I want a three-page double-spaced essay on why you want to be a writer. From those, I will choose thirty of you to continue with the course. Are there any questions?"

Whistles and wolf calls reigned but briefly. Silence restored, I looked for hands in the air. There were two. I nodded to the sweet young thing with a squeaky voice who asked, "May I have your babies?"

"My dear, the Board of Regents wouldn't approve. And more to the point," I lied, "I had a vasectomy several years ago. But thank you for asking."

A moan of regret swept across the crowd as a young football type stood for attention. "Dr. Stone," he asked, "Would you be gay with me for one night?"

More whistles of approval and stamping of feet. When able, I replied, "Sorry, laddy, but I fear that we would be driven from the Groves of Academe."

"Where are these groves I keep hearing about?" inquired my rejected lover.

"You're sitting among them at this time. Now, shall we turn our attention to the muse."

In a loud whisper, one of those present asked, "What's a muse?"

I shook my head as I said to myself, these are the darling idiots from the California public school system. Maybe one out of a hundred knows syntax from spandex. And that's how my teaching career began.

The essays that crossed my desk were pitiful and painful to read. I had a desire to mail them to our governor but then I recalled that he was equally as illiterate as my students. If I had any illusions about California public education I would have indulged in a nervous breakdown.

Eventually, the photograph of the Zozzy ad fell from the cafeteria wall, the billboard changed sponsors and my fame lasted perhaps two months. Even the animals grew bored with peace and quiet in our household. I sent out messages to the spirit of Absalom to come and amuse his lair.

Time passed and the opera season was upon us. I purchased a season ticket as usual. I refuse to go to the opera with any of my acquaintances as they cannot possibly live up to my expectations, nay my rules: no whispering, no applauding out of place, no bodily contact and no leaving before the curtain falls.

In relative calm, I attended a performance of La Boheme on a Saturday night and had a late appointment to meet Mario at a topless/bottomless bar in the Tenderloin as he had something to show me. I couldn't imagine what there was to see but decided to humor my best friend. I agreed to join him after the opera.

Certainly, I did not plan a denouement with the ballerina as I did not expect to ever see her again. I had worked hard to stop the pain of that loss and had no desire to damage fresh scar tissue. Finally, I had done my educational thing, matriculating ten years late but not necessarily ten years wiser. I had a new life that was not as exciting and mad as the old but I was at peace and slept well. I had no desire to meet any skeletons out of my past.

The main lobby of the Opera House sports a long cocktail bar and is always packed between acts as dignity and decorum are laid aside for one more shot before the next curtain. It is very much a business bar with no seating available.

We were between Acts II and III of La Boheme and the bar was surprisingly empty, a state that I attributed to a flat and fat soprano from Naples. In spite of these described circumstances, I found myself being shoved into a private party and face to face with Xanae.

"Tom," she said, as though we had lunched the day before, "How delightful to see you."

In a daze, I muttered words that I cannot remember, as I realized that her hand lay at rest on the arm of a dignified older man, obviously Greek, expensively dressed and with a diamond on his little finger. I knew that he was her husband, having read of their marriage in clippings sent to me anonymously in Selena's spidery script.

"This is my husband," she explained, "Dimitri Kannelos."

I knew him by reputation as he enjoyed the status of being a self-made millionaire with a fleet of fishing boats. The precious stones on Xanae's fingers he could afford. He insisted that I join his party for a late supper and as fast as I thought of excuses the quicker he countered my reluctance, which he did with great charm. I felt that he wanted his moment of victory and that she wanted her revenge as well and I compared myself to a beleaguered fox with the hounds nipping at its heels. Finally, I agreed, just to get rid of them, thinking that I would sneak from the opera house as the final curtain fell and that they would be unable to find me. Fortunately, they sat in orchestra seats and from my vantage point in the grand tier I could observe them covertly.

As the performance died its horrible death I fled down to the right aisle of the main floor that opens onto a small garden on the north side. Cold fog on my face brought me to a full alert and I decided to sneak toward the rear of the stage which abuts on

Franklin Street. This I did, and walked right into a black limousine waiting there for me, the door held open by one of her scowling brothers. Apparently, so I came to realize, her brothers were stationed at all possible exits but then what are six brothers for. As a reluctant guest, I entered the rear of the limo with what dignity I could muster.

Kanellos and party were greeted as royalty at the restaurant and nothing is more royal in San Francisco than money where most of the forebears were bricklayers, whores and scum. Bonhomme reigned, retsina flowed, toasts were made. Fully aware that all of those dignified Greeks were cognizant of my brief romance with Xanae, I was silently sincere in my gratitude for their deference to translations when something amusing had been said.

I wanted to die, to shrivel into nothingness in my seat but that was not to be, so I fixed a permanent smile on my face and braved the ordeal. Not one of the six brothers spoke to me during the entire meal.

I must say that Xanae's husband behaved in an admirable way and spoke to me often in fluent although heavily accented English. Toward the end of our meal, one of the ladies asked me what my occupation might be. Startled, I explained that I was a struggling writer. At this time, my gracious host said, "Are there any other kind?" To which I smiled and shrugged. My host then made the following statement, much to my surprise. Said Mr. Kannelos, "Being Greek, how could I care more or less for the man and his pen than for the man and his sword." Shaken to my toes, I nodded my thanks for his words.

Much to my consternation, it was my ballerina, now Dimitri's wife, who got tipsy and announced to none in particular, "Tom didn't love me enough." There was nothing to say and so I remained mute as quick-thinking guests changed the subject. With four short words, Xanae cursed me for years to come. In time, I came to think of her curse as my stigmata.

Some years later, and with no warning whatsoever, I came to accept the truth of Xanae's declaration and once I accepted I was no longer cursed. All that I loved about her was contrary to what I could endure and long relationships are primarily a case of endurance. I had my thing against large families of any ethnic or religious background. I hated the thought of marriage and pregnancies and births and christenings in any faith. I hated the guilt that families spread upon one another. I feared the primal instinct of togetherness.

As far as I know, all of my lovers are living out their lives and doing well without me. With thanks to Elizabeth Barrett Browning I will say to each and all of them: how did I love thee? Let me count the ways.

I left the Greeks at one o'clock and took a cab to the Topless/Bottomless bar on lower Turk Street where nude girls simulate sex with a barber pole. Mario was hardly aware that I had been so long in coming so enraptured was he with his surroundings.

"Man, have I got something to show you."

I wondered what it could be but Mario's genetic enthusiasm is a thing one learns to tolerate because he's such a lovable guy. With a nasty taste in my mouth from my encounter with Xanae, I wanted most to go home and was on the verge of pleading a headache when he hit my thigh with his knee and said, "Here she comes."

Ms. Reaves appeared in a garter, high heels and nothing more and commenced her simulated intercourse with the barber pole while the crowd went wild. She didn't look at us, she looked through us even when Mario tucked a twenty in her garter. Her performance was impressive but exotic dancer carried hyperbole to an extreme. Her writhing continued for roughly twenty minutes during which Mario among others screamed their approval. Still, she refused to recognize our presence. When she left the stage she was followed by a male. "She's turning tricks between shows," Mario explained. I think I'll go back and give her my Italian sausage.

"In which case, you'll be screwing a cross-section of San Francisco. I'd call that Russian Hill Roulette. Just keep it in your pants before you get caught with a good case of syphilis."

In some subtle way, I felt that my presence was a triumph for our Ms. Reaves. Maybe I read more than was there but she seemed to have found her metier and to hell with Dr. Thomas Richard Stone.

Mario grumbled a bit but deferred to my wishes and at bar closing time we made our way west to Foster's Cafeteria where the night people gather for food and rest with the rising of their neon sun. Musicians and singers from nearby clubs, jugglers and hypnotists who work cheap bars, all are there with pimps and their whores, junkies and drug peddlers, too, all the social rejects congregate at Foster's with red-rimmed eyes.

Afterward, we walked down deserted Market Street all the way to the Ferry Building and back to the garage where my car was parked. I sensed that Mario had something on his mind that he wished to share and that he was having difficulty breaking his code of silence. I felt his need for company and suggested that we go to the crest of Russian Hill and watch the sun come over the Berkeley hills, my established routine since I first came to the City.

As we leaned against the railing on that small circular spot Mario gave up his secret. "I've got to get out of the house," he blurted."

"Your mother?"

"Yeah. Each time I enter the house, she looks at my crotch and spits."

"That's because you aren't making babies."

"She's got ten grandchildren already and can't even remember their names."

"Your spreading of your seeds without harvest is an affront to la madre, the Holy Mother. You were born and raised a Catholic, you should know that. Your balls belong to la madre, don't you know?"

"I know I can't take it any longer."

"Then move out. The unwed child is not obligated by law to take care of an elderly parent. It's a custom and a convenience. Tell your brothers they'll have to put her in a convalescent home. The three of you own the restaurant; the three of you should share the cost of your mother's care. You've got to make the break. Move out, get your own pad. Find someone to love, someone who will never grow tired of your Italian sausage. Get a vasectomy so you can't make babies and then fuck your brains out."

"Where do I go? What do I do?"

"Are you happy at the restaurant and do you get along with your brothers?"

"Yeah. All I want is to get out of the house."

"Your brothers, they'll grumble a bit and try to make you feel guilty but be firm. They're living their lives, why shouldn't you? Come and stay with me and the beasties until you get reoriented."

"You mean it!"

"Yes. There's only one problem. You'll find yourself sleeping the with cats and dogs."

"I'll make out. And thanks. I love you for this."

"Por nada."

"When can I move in?"

"The sooner the better for you. You can pick up a key today."

We were silent for a spell as the Berkeley hills commenced to change color. I was startled when a serious Mario suddenly said, "I'm very proud of you."

"The myth or the man?"

"There you go, talking crazy again." Shortly thereafter, Mario seemed to remember something important which he wished to share. "I forgot to tell you, Selena is in the hospital and is near death. She has some kind of strange pneumonia and there's white stuff growing in her mouth. I heard it from an orderly at the hospital. He says that seven or eight gays have died from a similar disease and the authorities are trying to keep it quiet Nobody seems to know what the disease is or what causes it, in fact, it doesn't even have a name."

I watched the first rays of light appear on the eastern horizon while I decided to share my secret with Mario and having decided, I spoke in simple terms. "Three days ago, I woke to find Absalom's Star of David lying on the pillow beside me. At first, while half awake, I took it to be the one I wore thinking that somehow during sleep it had managed to remove itself from my body, an unlikely story at best. Sitting up in bed, I took off the chain that I wear and all doubts disappeared. I picked up the Star of David which went into the grave around my dear friend's neck and slipped it over my head. I knew it too well to have any doubts. I knew, also, that Absalom had returned it to me as a warning. In parapsychology, this phenomenon is called an apport."

"What's an apport?" asked the curious Mario.

"Tangible evidence that one has been visited by someone from the other side."

"You're too far out for me, kid."

"The spirit of Absalom hangs around the house most of the time. The dogs and cats have fun and games with him. You'll be staying in a haunted house. I hope you don't mind."

"I'll answer that later. Better your haunted house than my mother."

"Just think," I remarked, "We're standing here waiting for the sun to rise and you can be sure that others have stood here at this hour before us. It's fair to assume that two were standing here on April 18, 1906, waiting for the sun to clear the Berkeley hills, when at 513 AM, the earth shook. And from this pinnacle, they watched the City crumble. Imagine how scared they must have been and what conflicting emotions enveloped them. Did they run as fast as legs will respond to find if their homes were still standing, or were they simply transfixed, frozen into immovable statues as the fires began. Or did they travel through the rubble to Market Street in hopes of helping quell the fires only to find that the water mains had burst and that there was nothing to do except to watch it burn. Burn, baby, burn! All the way to Van Ness and in some spots even further."

"What would we do if at 513 AM, which is just three minutes away, what would you and I do if the earth shook and we saw the Transamerica building crumble as quietly as carefully stacked wooden matches? Firstly, we would be traumatized and unable to accept that once again our town had been reduced to trash."

"We would try to get to our homes and loved ones praying that all of them survived, If we had a radio with us, or one in the car, we would try to find the emergency broadcast station for instructions. Hopefully, the water mains would not burst this time. Hopefully, there would be no fire. Hopefully, no Bart trains would be caught under the Bay."

"The dead would be buried as quickly as possible and then we would learn to live among the debris of our new existence. Eventually, we would begin the monumental chore of rebuilding bigger and better than before."

"San Francisco is the eternal Phoenix. It will always survive. It was destined by the forces of nature to die and to be reborn at intervals which makes our hearts swell with pride each time we pause to enjoy the improbable beauty that surrounds us."

"I, too, have heard rumors of deaths from uncommon causes. I think that is why Absalom returned his Star of David to me. It was a warning of horrors to come. Many will die but in the end we shall survive."

"I think that most San Franciscans never leave even when they die. Like Absalom, their spirits remain. Why go to Heaven when you have Baghdad by the Bay!"

"And now, I have orders for you, amigo, keep that Italian sausage in your pants and be careful to whom you give it. Live for life. Death will find you when it's your time to go. I'm selfish, in case you didn't know. I don't want to bury you, I want you to bury me."

The End

MEMENTOS FROM THE SANTA FE OPERA

Since our second opera season together, I have been privy to some emotionally immature behavior on your part, to selfishness nonpariel, and to petty and vindictive conniving not associated with healthy adults.

Your childish tangents seem to have been borne out of the presence of two intimates of mine who happened to join me in Santa Fe during the opera season. For some strange reason they seem to have destroyed your sense of emotional security.

I was not and am not aware that you hold the keys to Santa Fe, or that the State of New Mexico is your personal fiefdom, subject to entry only at your whim. Neither do I think that you have a lease on the hotels and watering holes of the area. What I do think is that you are an opera goer who gives herself airs. Who follows me to Santa Fe is not your concern; those you bring are none of my business, and none but a member of the walking wounded would take upon themselves such an intolerable role.

After the fact, I assure you that my friends did not travel to Santa Fe to see you or to interfere with your stringently structured social calendar, about which they could care less. They, and myself, are not accustomed to buying dowagers, maitre d's and waiters for lunch, unless sex was in the offing, and I happen to know that you didn't get laid for your money. So much for bad investments!

My decision to attend the Wagner Festival in Seattle, the following summer, was a matter of no personal affront to anyone, and if some cretin chose to play the role of the rejected then that was their decision and a matter over which I have no control and no interest.

What intrigues me most are your Santa Fe machinations. By ignoring me, in your planning for a third season, you seem to have thought that I might never get tickets without your assistance. I know the way to Santa Fe, I know how to order opera tickets, and my checks don't bounce. I have had splendid seats since they came on the market. Indeed, it may turn out that you will find me sitting alongside you upon occasion, an occurrence which could possibly drive you into a purple straitjacket.

Your behavior falls under the aegis of socially unacceptable and I suggest that you stay away from me henceforth, otherwise. I may find it necessary to wrap that silly purse around your fat neck.

Sincerely,
(Surprisingly, this letter to la Loca brought to an end a non-productive relationship)

HOW TO LOSE FRIENDS AND ALIENATE
PEOPLE - Letters to Lady Pamela

Oh, exquisite day, I am going to say it!

One cannot and should not love or loathe a country or people, or culture, just because they are THEY. My slipping of the dictum, to some extent, extends to the Irish, whose blood runs in my veins. Fortunately, the Moorish blood in the Black Irish, plus one quarter Cherokee from my paternal grandmother, plus another quarter from the Cajun in her DNA, saves me from being one hundred per cent Irish. Of the Irish, I will say in passing, A PLAGUE ON BOTH OF YOUR HOUSES.

The above is not an hypothesis as there is too much data to support the theorem that the purer the Spanish blood in Hispanics the higher the status, the greater the accumulation of power, the greater the purloining of the public purse and the greater the ethnic arrogance. I assess this overdone sense of self-importance to a deep-seated hatred of the other half of their corpuscles be they Indian, Filipino, Aztec, Mayan or whatever. Where Mexico and most of Central and South America are concerned, the mestizo is the majority of the population. And in such countries as Mexico, for example, the mestizo remains on the short end of the stick regardless of propaganda to the contrary. The Castilian blood, that personal portion of it, remains the bellweather of status.

Into this Mexican time capsule goes the yanqui, the gringo, primed by economic and cultural explosives; enter the Ugly American turista often and over long periods of time. Why? Because this is where the gringo can buy a sense of superiority based on exchanged rates, U.S. dollars vis-à-vis the Mexican peso.

Alas, one finds no evidence that you contributed to them or they to you. Unless one is of a mind to grant the translation of some play from Spanish to English, in pursuit of self-aggrandizement, or the transfer of pesos for an assignation. One sees in this the chilling prophecy of the essence seeking itself for a continuation of karma begun and repeated perhaps through many lives.

What distresses me most about the translation bit is this dichotomy in words and behavior. If you could not correct (proof read) perhaps a hundred lines of Mexican Spanish then how in the hell would your knowledge of said language give you the credentials for the translation of a book or play? This, too, is a puzzlement.

I have had the questionable luck to know three congenital liars much too closely. Oh, I've known many more, but they were sufficiently removed so that their blackness could not taint my aura. Surprisingly, I have never thought of you as one of the congenital three but after some strenuous brainwork I have had to accept that you are one, too. From life experiences with such afflictions it seems that yours are the lies of temporary self-aggrandizement the lies of a sociopathic aided and abetted by alcoholism but when I put the four of you into the same pod and shake it well, you fall in place nicely.

The translation caper leads me to suspect that you insist on getting caught in such falsehoods which may be a part of the psychological pattern. If you are incapable of proofing the elemental Spanish in question then I must debate your presumption in translating someone's creative endeavors. Personally, I cannot read myself into any of this, for I lie with reason aforethought and don't saute the falsehoods in subversive sauces. This is my definition of the difference between one who lies for psychological reasons and one who lies for expediency. No moral inferences need be drawn between the two for that is not the subject under discussion. If it were, then I would say that my definition of morality is a concern for my fellow persons. By this definition (of morality) then you congenital liars would turn out to be frightfully immoral.

I suspect that my last impressions of you will contain these bits: you and Marilyn Monroe had much in common, as I've said before. And she was common while you started out with class and a good education. Where you and Marilyn join at the hip is when she held aloft her copy of Proust and pretended to read while the book was held upside-down. Poor dumb, drunk and

66

stoned doxie thinking that essence can be bought at the marketplace. From my point of view, you were Marilyn's sister under the skin. I base this on you deification of all things Spic. And for comparable reasons.

Mexico has a rich, tragic and brutal history and it continues today in the identical cycle that produces torture, graft, political instability and a people who scream about love of country while sacking their cash for trips to the nearest U.S. bank. Mexicans are nowhere more cruel than to their fellow beings, especially to the mestizos and Indians. Perhaps one should speak of all latin countries as being cursed thusly. An additional curse comes from the Church.

Flip the peso, however, and there can be found the magnificent dignity, the charm, the outpouring of affection, the emotionality of a people that gave meaning to such words as compadre, among others. I see them as star-crossed people who are too busy destroying themselves to correct their misdirected sense of history and self.

I am racked by the Mexicans' bloody past, our taking of their land and by fear of the bloodletting yet to come. I worship their music, their art and their artists, their extremes of wealth and poverty torture me. Their physical beauty is forevermore striking. I love these people for myriad reasons not the least being the dignity and courage of the peon to survive and endure and endure.

I am less than sanguine about what you took out of Mexico, Central and South America during your years of travel, the most tangible positive being a favorable exchange of dollars for! It's not what you do that annoys me as much as it is your efforts at deification of it. One fears, my dear, that you travel on false papers.

Dear Lady P:

You had all the answers but, alas, you didn't have the questions.

In your small-time way, you pervert our language as well as most people do. A case in point! For almost nine years to the

67

day (of my opera fling in Seattle), my ill-concealed disgust with you has been fed back to me as MY PARANOIA. Perhaps the truth was more than your delicate condition could sustain. And it is of no lasting consequence to me.

As I have explained before, and for your educational growth: there are two types of sociopathic personalities. I suggest you drag your lazy ass from a bar stoll and get thee to a library, there to corrcct the fallacy in your thinking.

We are in a four-day seige of high temps, 110 to 114 degrees. It is as dry as a perfect martini. I am thriving on it. But then you don't sweat, which is another of your many myths.

I have written to J & J and Owens and offered them a copy of the manuscripts, early drafts soon to be discarded. J & J never got to read part two of LAND OF THE GREEN GOLD and Owens was too niggardly to pay $60 for a copy. Owens has a short-lived interest in all things, so one expects nothing of longevity from that source. As for myself, I have no sentimental interest in early drafts. I'll leave that to Mozart and Shakespeare, although there is no evidence that Shakespeare had any. And! I have written to my asociopathic <u>seester</u> and asked if she would like to read the book ere we all go byebye. I explained to her that LOTGG is full of fucks, shits and all the rest and not to read it if it will cause in infarct or something. I shall be amused by her reaction as I perceive that it will be roughly tatamount to reaction from the Pope upon receiving an invitation to view a porno film.

Buttercup called last Sunday, to announce that her father died the Saturday before. ABA asked if she were going to the funeral. There is no point in going back, she moaned, he gave his body to the medical school (Syracuse University). She wanted to <u>wisit</u> (her spech impediment, not mine) but ABA had been warned to keep her away from me, so her told her that I was fasting and purging for a colonoscopy and, being ABA, he threw a lot of garnee on the plate. Well, I guess you don't want company, Bcup moaned.

You seem to lose and overview where my Veterans Disability Compensation is concerned. I'd like a <u>waise</u> but not a <u>woom</u> <u>wif</u> <u>wubber</u> walls.

On your continuing interest in my anatomy: no, I was not circumcized for reasons that probably had to do with home delivery by a country doctor, while Aunt Lora, with both the black and the white hairs in her mole quivering, joined black Georgia, my mother's mammy, in the deliverance of boiling water up the stairs to the attic room where I was shot forth into the same family for the second time. When I was six or seven, my father took me to a doctor in regards to the status of my prepuce where the question was: should we or shouldn't we. All I can recall is the mortal shame of having to drop my pants before my father and a doctor. Nothing came of it and the prepuce went back by itself about my ninth year when my sexual activity began. My prepuce has never covered the glans since. I suppose this had to do with (1) prolific sexual activity and (2) the beeg head on my cock. What else would you like to know on that subject?

Is the cunt who is moving in with Buttercup the same one who lambasted her for being queer, you ask. Yes! When I gasped upon hearing, she started screaming about being put down. Surely you need no further evidence of Bcup's scrambled brains.

The Howard Kleinberg (Cox News Service) article on Hemingway and other things does not turn me on. But neither did Closet Queen Ernest who was certainly the number one quack of letters of our closing century. Had he written long or short, Ernest would have made no change in my contempt for his adolescent attempts. Short is not necessarily good, as you seem to presume, while long is not necessarily bad. It is the content that counts and how the material lends itself to a chosen length. OLD MAN AND THE SEA was not quite short enough but it was a pretentious bore at any length. I know why Hemingway blew his head off: he could no longer endure being a classic fraud. Sometimes, so I think, many frauds from various millieux should take a lesson from Ernest, yourself included.

Tennessee Williams' only novel, a novella really, by name THE ROMAN SPRING OF MRS. STONE, is perhaps his best work. Without your having to look it up, a novella implies that it is short and that the material fits the length to perfection.

Inadvertently, I may have found my next inspiration. As soon as LOTGG is out of my hands, I may write another version of ROMAN SPRING devoted exclusively to aging queens who have money but little else forever traveling but staying nowhere, flotsam on a 747, never belonging to anyone, time or place, empty, unloved and unloving, scared but with hope still alive, in the manner of Mrs. Stone, unable to keep themselves from trying to create essence where none exists. You and Miss Jessel should make fine protagonists for what will be a SHORT novel. I believe that I am inspired.

6/29/90

Lady Pamela:

This is (next to) THE LAST WORD ON GUESTS AND GUESTING.

In our pixillated version of OLD ACQUAINTANCE we seem to have embarked on a disparate third act. As you are much too sensitive to the nuances of human behavior to write with objectivity, I'll do it for you.

I was conditioned early to Shaw's dictum on fish and guests, long before I knew that GBS existed. I believe that it was GBS who made the immortal statement but if not, I'm sure you'll correct me. Be this as it may, my negative conditioning to the state of guesting began with the crash of 1929 when, at that time we were forced to return to the Dunn house for roof and succor, both to be provided by two aunts who claimed to love us. This affection did not extend to our father who was allowed to sleep in the house with his family but was forced to walk several miles a day for meals at his mother's table.

Legally, we had an inherited interest in the Dunn mansion, if we may used the term loosely, as in the will of my grandfather said property was left to Liz until such time as she married or died. That Lizzie Dunn would never marry was a forgone conclusion among townfolk as she had never entertained a swain, not even on the green porch swing in the presence of a parent. It is equally a forgone conclusion that none but Doctor Seale, the village doctor, had ever heard of Freud. It would take

70

time for the precious grandson to reach an age of reason wherefrom the name of Freud would have meaning, and it was at this time that the precocious sibling came to understand that his Aunt Liz would have been a lesbian in a later time and place. Precious offspring reasoned further that if his hell-fire-and-brimstone grandfather had been able to comprehend the intricacies of Freudian sexuality Liz would have been driven from the house in sackcloth and ashes. As for the Dunn girls times three, ditzy birds out of their cage, life boiled down to what mama said and what papa and Aunt Rushia said and no court of law would ever change their unwritten rules of behavior. In time, all of these delicious possibilities drove precious grandson to under ground research for the source of his grandfather's wealth, and accumulation of cash and land that a country drugstore could never produce. What grandson found were deeds of land made to his grandfather…deeds from both blacks and whites…sharecroppers who lost their land and personal possessions when they were unable to repay their benefactor better known as Thomas Richard Dunn.

We stayed in that house as unwelcome guests for perhaps three years, or until my sister was scheduled to return from the hospital following surgery that saved not only her life but her leg as well. At that time, dear Aunt Liz wept a bucketful as she refused to allow her nine year old niece back into the house. Years later, Liz died of starvation in that same abode. Fate is sometimes just.

Years later, our venal Aunt Lora drove my sister and brother-in-law from the property after they had fed her for several years. In time, and after a life of gorging, Lora was given a colostomy. In the residence of a neighbor, she died of post-surgical complications. Fate is sometimes just.

Prior to Lora's death, my mother had gone to that great big church in the sky…Protestant, of course…where she could be told how pretty she was. If this didn't happen, then Lou Annie's Protestant Heaven became her Protestant Hell. I trust that this silly simpering southern bitch is forced to sit under a hair dryer until her next reincarnation.

These remembrances reaffirm the history of my early and negative conditioning to the state of being a guest.

Guesting is a polite aphorism for the indigent who are without roof, bed and board, those who are forced to depend upon the kindness of strangers to get them by.

My guesting has been done among a select few and all of them you know, at least from endless reportage if not in person. As a child, I doted on guesting, of course, for guesting is bred into southerners. We took annual trips to see the Dunns, or to visit with our paternal grandparents, aunt and uncles. These trips I associate with the holiday seasons when I could be among those relatives I loved while simultaneously stuffing my young stomach to the point of nausea. These were the times before the true nature of the Dunn girls became apparent to the fledgling pubescent that was myself.

Making a fast forward in time, Carlota welcomed me with open arms after the death of her mother who held a formidable dislike for all people named Shields. Her reasons were less than opaque. Firstly, my second cousin had impregnated her second daughter and, secondly, I had deserted my mother. As she had taken her complaisant second son as a husband, sans sex, she looked upon me as a threat to her security. Would that I had been able to untie that Gordian Knot, that Oedipus Rex complex that led inexorably to her sibling's predestined destruction. But back to sunnier days with Carlota, a time when I was too naive to see that hers was not an altruistic gesture, her y'all come was a cry of desperation, and even when I perceived the truth, I was still happy to be there as she could be great fun and hysterically amusing while listening to Butterfly and weeping copiously as she ironed those ubiquitous white shirts.

The rest is history. She found Teddy- poo who was a fast fuck on the stairs and down she went into the tube of degredation. Years later, I was able to accept that Carlota became what she wanted to be. Regardless, I miss her and resent her for having abandoned me.

Louis was a strange case, strange in childhood, stranger in his adult years, or perhaps I was able to perceive him more clearly with adult eyes. At his insistence, I guested from time to time, both before, during and after Joan. Yet he didn't seem to know what to do with me when I was there and I was acutely uncomfortable. The curtain descended and I walked away, sans comment, after he mocked his need for me on the night of Joan's passing. Adieu, Louis.

La Loca came into my life upon my return to college after a ten year hiatus. Like those of her desperate nature, invitations were tossed about with abandon in the hope that some might be accepted. Those few times when I partook were traumatic to an extreme. The denouement to this ill-fated pas de deux grew out of our shared experiences in Santa Fe and her amateurish fanagling following our last season there together. Adios, La Loca, and good riddance!

Loretta was generous with invitations to Rob's house but eventually Rob drove her and her piano from the premises. This indicated a certain bit of good sense from Rob and he was to be congratulated. In the lives of Loretta and Rob, at that time, I must have been seen as something special from among their list of acquaintances. What I felt like was a free-loader and, at that time, I could have paid my way. Now I wonder why I didn't.

La Booboo solved the guesting problem by remaining in her rabbit hutch at 999 Bush Street. She got the vapors if I came to town unemployed.

From my ill-fated sagas as a guest, I have drawn what is perhaps a slightly warped decision: those most ill-equipped to be hostesses are those most prone to toss around invitations. Shall we call them 'hostesses without the mostest'? In their cavalier manner they made the grandstand play; they invited guests only to find out that they did not possess the emotional equipment to behave as proper hostesses should.

Some, so I have discovered, with no names mentioned, send out invitations for sado-massochistic reasons. Three-day old Shavian fish in the house gives them the chance to play the put upon paragon of altruism while altruism had nothing to do with it. They asked for and received the barrel of cod that arrived smelling at their door.

In the saga of guesting one cannot ignore Lady Blanche...who was no lady...who spent long periods as your

73

guest, although you 'were never really that close', or as you said, stretching a point of redundancy in a recent tome. What a pity I didn't keep your long laments about the Arkansas monkey on your back, in this case, Blanche, to whom you were not really close, yet close enough to feed her drugs for her habit. Had I kept your written wails, I could mail them back to you at this rancid hour. But like Mumsie, you have rewritten history to conform to your moods and needs and resent vehemently any inference to logic which might inflame your uvula.

With all the honesty that I can muster at this witching hour I must say that there wasn't much left of Blanche to be 'close to' by the time I met her. But let history record that Blanche guested long and often and she was a lousy cook. You carried on at great length about your inability to pry her fingers from your door, even with pliers and torch. My lasting memory of Blanche has to do with her physical machinations when getting out of bed. From her paranoid-schizophrenic mind she had convinced herself that by sliding from the sheets at an oblique angle, she could de-emphasize the width of her hips.

On many occasions when I guested with you alone I relished the occasion. These were periods of interpersonal fulfillment, or so it seemed to me. Apparently, I presumed too much: I was an intruder who did not know his place, manners or duties, those that befit his station. Your most recent rewriting of our history destroys my last illusion but there is a certain freedom in having none left. Your perversion of facts makes Buttercup's demand that I 'do floors' seem positively refreshing.

My point has been made, now to the summation. I regret having ever been a house guest with anyone at any time, and while I remain grateful for emergency shelter and subsistance, I question the motives of my various hostesses. As for the recalcitrant recipient of such largesse, there is always a core of resentment which is the seed of revolution.

Alas, I am too old to go to war and the only movement that has ever interested me is a healthy B. M.

I presume that Blanche received her share of letters bewailing my presence in your house, just as I received mine bewailing hers.

After finding this letter and reacquainting myself with its contents. I have reached two conclusions. (1) Anything said subsequently on the subject (by me) was superfluous and redundant and (2) you and Lizzie Dunn had a great deal in common.

Lady Pamela:

Had I been asked, I would have suggested that you wait until there is a vaccine for THAT disease before banging your friend, the former whorelet, in the baths of Santo Domingo. THIS one does not have much in common with good old GC or syphillis; you can only get it once. Having seen the back-to-back programs on AIDS (PBS) last night, one can only hope that you come up with the good sense to keep your genitalia in your pants. As I have history of how foolish you can be, I am concerned.

Roget's many words on the meaning and usage of insular and insularity are there for anyone to read. Your suggestion that they are <u>obscure</u> does not raise my opinion of your intelligence one iota. Any idiot who can read can find them, the words in Roget. Perhaps this great reference source to language hurts your head. What you did was to make an unfortunate choice of words that were not suitable to the subject nor to the point that you wished to make. You can choke on it, either in the throat or up the ass, take your pick. I GIVE YOU CREDIT FOR NOTHING and do not concur with you in any way. But as Mumsie used to say, you want credit, which may be your ego problem or, at least, part of it. So I am giving you credit here and now. I give you credit for your ongoing efforts and your insistence on making a fool of yourself.

Recently, I read a column by one of our talking head agony sisters, said letter written by a mother regarding her daughter's relationship with another female. It seems that ditzy daughter had gone ape over another woman thus endangering a happy home with husband and daughter. According to the aggrieved mother, the two women were not gay, they just went ape over one another. If the reader can buy this hypotheses then perhaps we are all subject to buying the Panama Canal but, for the sake of continuity, we shall pretend. Talking Head Agony Sister suggests that the wife/mother was indulging in what psychiatrists call displacement behavior. This mental state is alleged to occur when a person avoids dealing with life's problems by concentrating, often compulsively, on other people and their activities. Agony Sister explains that many people find it easier and more gratifying to solve other people's problems than to face their own.

After reading this letter and the response on replacement behavior, I wrote to Agony Sister with your case in mind. Never fear your anonymity was protected. In her response, Agony Sister wishes me to advise you that obfuscation and transferrence are part of the displacement behavior pattern. Weepy One further suggests that personalities addicted to this type of behavior syndrome show patterns of sociopathic tendencies. Admitting to any need, any imperfection, would bring down their house of cards (self-deception) in which the subject lives. Crying Critter suggests further that those addicted to displacement behavior are the ultimate bores. Weepy One was quite diplomatic in her response, which I am not, and was intrigued by the efforts to which a practicioner of displacement behavior will go to hold tight to their status quo, whatever that might be. She referred, in particular, to your denigration of Roget and the Thesaurus to authenticate a point.

I thought that you were going to Santo Domingo to see your dear friend, the one with the beeg cock, but your departure letter brought food for thought. I refer to the fact that you were to need a few days to yourself before looking up your friend. This leads me to conclude that your sole reason for this trip was because it was cheap. Would it have not been even cheaper to stay at home in your ebony barrio? Your need for three days to get yourself together runs perilously close to the machinations of the late and loony Blanche Lewis.

TIPS ON GOING TO JAIL

A friend once remarked that I would find meaningful experiences in Hell and that he would look forward to reading about them. Not long ago, I spent a night in Hell, or as close as I care to come to that metaphorical place. I spent my night not at the Devil's Hilton; mine was spent in the Vista Detention Center better known as the Vista jail.

I was arrested on a Thursday afternoon and arrived at the Vista Detention Center at approximately 3:30 P.M. That I had been charged with an alleged crime held less significance than the fact that I was there!

Once in jail, I was forced to strip. A cursory inspection of my orifices was made. Later in the evening, I was forced to strip again. It was all part of the System.

Mixed with the horror of my twenty-two hours in the 'tank' were fleeting moments of exhaltation. Youths sharing my cell came to the aid of the 'old man' when a nurse refused medication as the old man did not rise when she called his name. At possible risk to themselves the young men protested verbally to the angel in white who was straight out of those old Nazi war movies.

An aging Marine Sergeant, drunk and very much an alcoholic, joined our group. He was there to serve four months for a parole violation. "You're no jailbird," he said to me. We embraced at the time of my departure. I don't know his name and will never see him again but he is a part of my life.

Wherever man is incarcerated, brutality lies restlessly under the skin, be it in the Vista jail, a psychiatric ward or a military academy. College educated deputies with mod hairdos are not immune to the contamination. Both the prisoner and his jailer become victims of the System. Yet, as jails go, Vista Detention Center must rank as a posh resort.

When I was called to report to the Sheriff's Station in Fallbrook I thought I was going in for a chat. Little did I realize that I was to be arrested. Street-wise, I am not smart. You learn fast in jail.

Lesson Number One! Always get arrested early in the day and never on weekends. On an average, it takes two to ten hours to post bail and get out, if all goes well. Not only is your body explored, so is your life history. Somewhere, Big Brother has a computer that tells <u>all</u>. Not until the computer reports that you are clean will you be released, even if bail has been arranged. I speak of the novice caught in the System, of course. The recidivists work on a different level.

I had money for bail but there were pertinent documents in safe keeping and banks don't open at the convenience of desperate people. Lesson Number Two! Keep copies of legal documents at home. Lesson Number Three! Keep cash in the house for bail purposes, if you can afford to do so. But you're never going to be in jail, you say. Who knows? I didn't

Affluence is not an automatic key to release. Parents of a young man booked simultaneously with myself came to the jail with a check for six thousand dollars bail in full for their son's release. Personal checks are not accepted. Neither is Visa nor Mastercard.

The recidivists move in and out of jail with ease for they have become an integral part of the System. Among this group you will find the perennial drunks, petty thiefs and those incorrigibles who seem to have some sado-massochistic need for incarceration. Among others who fall into this group are the whores with pimps who facilitate their release so that the girls can get back on the streets. Then there are members of organized crime in close contact with lawyers who carry fat wads of cash. Jail is not for the middle-class citizen.

For those unfamiliar with jail jargon 'tank' is a euphemism connoting a holding cell where prisoners are kept until further disposition can be made. Those in the tank may be waiting for bail, such as myself, some may be in transit, while others may be waiting for more permanent quarters in the facility of their arrest.

After we were fingerprinted and mugged (photographed) we were moved further into the bowels of the tank area. This occurred at approximately seven o'clock on the night of incarceration. Three of us started our night together in our new digs, a tank approximately nine by twelve with three plexi-glass walls. Ambiance came from one wooden bench, a stainless steel open toilet and a cold and dirty cement floor. The toilet was decorated with apple cores and remnants of jailhouse sandwiches. Having been tossed a couple of these goodies, I learned quickly why most end up in the tank toilets.

During the night we grew from three to nine in number. Those most adaptable threw themselves on the cold cement floor and slept. Those less adaptable, like myself, sat on the wooden bench and dozed, or stood and gave others a chance to sit.

I was intrigued by the camaraderie that developed among our disparate group. I was told that this does not occur in more permanent detention facilities where ethnic power blocks are formed instantly.

Among the human sardines in our pexiglass tank was a latino who was no stranger to jail. One of our original three, he removed his shirt so that we might take a look at the fresh scar on his back. According to him, his lung had been cut in half during a fight. Surgery saved his life.

During the early morning hours this fellow grew nauseous. Having not eaten in hours, his retch came out as brackish foam. Apparently, the physical exertion caused him to vomit blood, two mouthsful of it. I know, I was watching. When I saw the blood I called to the nurse who happened to be nearby. Under protection of a deputy she entered the tank to inspect his residue. Among apple cores and uneaten sandwiches blood was not easy to see. "I don't see any blood," she complained, glaring at me, "I bleed more than that when I brush my teeth. Next time, spit in toilet tissue so I can see." The fact that there was no toilet tissue in the cell did not impress her. With another glare in my direction she departed.

It occurred to me, after the fact, that had I been a younger man I might have been stripped and thrown into solitary confinement for meddling in jailhouse affairs. As I said, you learn fast in jail.

I cannot speak for humanity but in my case tension and trauma dehydrate my body. After seven hours without water, or liquid of any kind, my mouth and tongue were stuck together. By then, the bailbondsman had visited and I knew that I would not be released until the following day. On our way back to the tank I begged the deputy for water. Roughly an hour later, a plastic jarful and a few styrofoam cups were brought to our tank. Water has never been so precious, although I questioned the sanitary conditions under which I drank.

Our Fight or Flight Syndrome takes myriad forms of expression. A migraine is my escape from stimuli overload. Without heavy medication, the migraine becomes worse than the shock the mind hopes to escape. My body doesn't know the difference, of course, it responds to message units from my brain. Fortunately, I was able to apply hypnosis training and stopped the migraine before it consumed me.

Through the long night we unfortunates sat or stood or slept and adjusted according to our conditioning. I looked at my clothing and realized how filthy I had become in a few short hours. Lesson Number Four! Always wear old clothes to jail. You'll look silly in a tux or yachting attire.

I have a built-in timer that rings once I have passed a point of no return. When I get the signal I know that I can make it the rest of the way, regardless of the destination. Through the night I watched the office clock, the slowest clock I have ever watched. About four o'clock on that wretched Friday morning, the nine in our tank were told to strip. Our personal clothing was replaced by jailhouse togs. Afterward, we were marched to a storage room where thin mattresses and one blanket were issued to each. From there, we were separated into three groups. Each group was assigned to a different module.

Module is a fancy name for a series of cells built around a community area. For the first time in over twenty-four hours I was able to lie down and stretch out. I pulled the blanket up to my chin, placed a folded towel over my eyes and slept lightly through a din of television, radio and the clanging of metal doors.

Through the rear of the module there was a recreation area. About nine o'clock I took cognizance of the electronic locking of my cell door so that prisoners from other areas might pass through. For that brief time, I was locked in a cell by myself. I learned the meaning of claustrophobia in one easy lesson.

10:00 A.M. Friday. I was taken back to a conference room for a second meeting with the bailbondsman. The necessary paperwork was completed and signatures affixed. I was assured that I would be released shortly.

The System makes sure that you will never forget your first night in jail, and for a reason, they hope you will be so impressed that you'll never return. I was impressed. As I was returned to my cell I took note of a certain change in attitude from the guards in attendance. I had been given the treatment; I was on my way out. Less harshness might be condoned.

10:00 to 11:00 A.M. This was the longest hour of my jail experience. My cellmates knew that bail had been arranged and that I would be released soon. There were smiles from those who had not spoken to me previously. On the collective face I found mixed emotions: sadness for self; joy for me. I felt guilty when I left.

I was returned to a holding tank...that limbo where you're not quite in and not quite out...and there I met again two young men from among the nine with whom I spent the night. These thoroughly middle-class and decent youths had been caught smoking a joint while watching the surf. During our long night in the tank they were afraid of being raped. They had been given back their personal clothing and were dressed for release. I stripped again and swapped jail garb for my personal attire which was shoved to me through a barred window. From thereon, it was a matter of waiting.

Noon Friday. The three of us made our final walk to freedom. We signed for the return of personal property, the last door swung open and we found ourselves back in a world that seems so far away from the inside.

As I walked toward the lobby of the Vista Detention Center I glanced at my image in a mirror and recoiled at what I saw. Then recoil turned into a shrug. So I looked like a poorly embalmed cadaver. I was free...at least for a time. That Friday afternoon was one of the most intensely lived of all the days of my life.

What did I do when I got out? Well, what would you expect from a former restaurant critic! I dined sumptuously on Mandarin Cuisine.

During the period when prisoners are in holding tanks communication with the outside is limited to visits from attorneys, bailbondsmen or members of the clergy. Family and friends may claw their fingers bloody against the walls of the System but they cannot get to you. Via the bailbondsman, on his first visit, I sent word to play it cool, as there was nothing to be done until the next day. Hopefully, my message would save loved ones from further guilt trips. In a few hours, I had learned that the System must run its course but, for those waiting on the outside, there is little or no frame of reference for such quick study.

I came home to a rainsoaked weekend which kept me inside. I would try to sleep but kept waking with the shakes. Aftershock and a most logical depression attacked me. Not until the early hours of Monday was I able to look at my circumstances with some objectivity. Whether innocent or guilty, as charged, I might spend some of my mature years in prison. What will be, will be, I decided, and made up my mind that I would not go quietly into a cell.

How did I land in jail? Well, here it is, far out and sound: I needed background material for a novel I was writing on the avocado country of North San Diego County. In order to study the life style of the natives, and to absorb local color, I became employed as a part-time clerk in a liquor store where I could work undercover as a literary spy. Subsequently, I was accused of embezzlement and arrested.

The novel is finished but I still ponder the question: is truth really stranger than fiction? But there's another story.

SO YOU WANT TO BE A WRITER

Easter Sunday is approaching and the house is open on this balmy night. Tellie has been atrocious as it usually is the day before and the day after a holiday. There was nothing to watch except religious services and so I typed manuscript into the late evening hours while small flying things were consumed by the typewriter which served to remind me that I could never endure the tropics because of those creepy crawling creatures yet here I live on the Mojave which has its share of them. The difference is the absence of humidity.

Earlier in the evening, as Easter dawned around the globe, I grew weary of watching the Pope do his yearly washing and kissing of the feet. Yet I shouldn't be too harsh with His Holiness as I have enjoyed a foot fetish or two, in my time.

The book was finished before I went to Vietnam to write tripe for a west coast paper which would never publish what was truth even if one were stupid enough to record it. So I shrugged away my integrity and cribbed from daily military press releases and seldom left the comforts of Saigon knowing damned good and well that I only took the assignment in order to avoid the marketing of the book. Coming home was an anti-climax for in my mind I never left.

When assailed about the book still unpublished I explained to my enamorata that I couldn't find the rough draft of my mailing piece which I had put away for safe keeping before my departure for foreign assignment. She was not impressed with my euphemism for filing and with no effort at all, she pulled the hidden draft from my favorite file marked Human Sexuality. In disgust, she waved the draft before my face. Cruel are the fates that bring the artistic soul into an alliance with a shrew.

A literary rule of thumb is this: if it gets cold, and you don't gag on it, then you may have something going. Reading the resurrected draft was an omen: the time had come and so I set to and polished my mailing piece to perfection, which is a doube entendre if ever I wrote one. The burnished bulletin was supposed to tell disinterested people what the novel was about.

83

And what it is not about, equally a terrible task. In a frenzy, I overwrote and went on eating and gin binges, I moaned and carried on and got pissed at my soulmate on numerous occasions. Finally, she sat me down and spoke her magic words that can only be learned from a Jewish mother.

"Forget the book," she railed, "It's over and done with You've had it; a long pregnancy is kaput and you've spawned a monster, so I suggest that you put on your other hat, the schlach chapeau you wore with such elan when you were a hack doing all that trashy stuff for business houses. If you could turn out all that crud and live with yourself, plus the garbage you sent home from Saigon, then surely you have the necessary lack of character to deal with editors, agents and publishers. Remember what Uncle Sidney once told you many times: don't let cunts push you around. Just think of them sitting on the pot doing their business, he said, and you'll know how to handle bimbos. What a blessing that dear Uncle Sid didn't live to see bimbos with both indoor and outdoor plumbing. Such a sight would have broken his heart. Regardless of plumbing, I might add, each feeds at the same trough and is eaten alive by greed while none of them has an attention span longer than thirty seconds."

The source of my inspiration and strength paused long enough to pour herself a glass of my cheap Dago red, which she only drinks when she hates me. Standing center of our patio, she proclaimed: "You have the hook in their mouths with your first page," as she quoted author to author, "Fruit hangs heavy, like the testicles of man, ready for the harvest. Thus was the Aztec name inspired...the ahuacatle...and with it the legend of aphrodisia. Once it dawns on your readers that the testicles of man inspired the ahuacatle of the Aztec, the aguacate of the Spanish and the avocado in English, turistas by the planeloads will arrive in avocado country to see for themselves how the fruit grows in pairs, one slightly higher than the other, just like yours, my pet, and most will lament that theirs aren't as heavy as the green pods. That any male would want to carry around an extra pound between his legs is machismo gone mad."

When the mailing piece was finished, proofed and printed, I began the sordid chore of sending out inquiries which I equate with selling Avon door-to-door. What happened thereafter is that I slid back into the pits of the business and found that all of my prototypals…from readers to editors to publishers to producers to agents…were just where I had left them. Only a few faces had changed but not a mentality. This explains why I lay awake at three o'clock on an Easter morning beset by wide-awake nightmares.

Through a freaky friend who had a thespian lover in NYC I managed to get the ear of someone at an agency who was tongue-washed on my behalf. I have no idea why this sacrifice was made and am probably better off for it. Such offerings are seldom if ever of an altruistic nature, certainly not in the world of the arts where the giving of one's body is the expected down payment. The Hispanics call it la mordida, which is much more explicit then in English. Apparently, this sexual duet generated much praise for my book from the subalterns and gained me an interview with the Top Bagel at the agency.

The thought of going to New York sent my blood pressure soaring and activated dormant colitis, to name a few and, upon arrival, I was in a state of depression. I've never liked the place since my first visit there when I was twenty-one and impressionable.

I reached the Agency on schedule and was kept waiting for twenty minutes, which is standard procedure when dealing with unknowns and undesirables which follows a geometric equation that things equal to the same thing are equal to each other. Roughly translated, this means that all unknowns are undesirables, When Miz Secretary told me that I could enter the holy place, her words came out as though Moses were waiting on the other side to part the Red Sea or, in this case, the East River.

I found myself is a modestly decorated office done in spartan good taste. Behind a grayish desk sat this corpulent man dressed in black. His spectacles were set in heavy black frames and I suspected that an expensive dye job had been done on the thinning hair. Native New Yorkers speak in a manner that makes me think that they're about to toss their lunch and this one was no exception. He indicated that I sit without shaking hands and inquired if I would like coffee. I agreed. He buzzed and announced coffee for one, explaining to me that coffee in the morning gave him gas. Why did I get the feeling that I was supposed to feel responsible?

Top Bagel was totally uncommunicative and to cover the loud silence I found myself making small talk. Finally, he said, "Your book needs much work. But this agency cannot take on any new writers at this time."

I waited for some sort of elucidation but none came and so I spoke. "I am pleased with the book as written. Were I less than pleased, I would still be working on it." About this time, I received a premonition that he had not read the book, which gave me a sense of freedom to say whatever I chose and so I said: "Did the desert scenes with the fornicating camels come off well? I had a bitch of a time getting that on paper, as I have never had the pleasure of observing camels in heat."

Top Dog clasped a heavy hand to his throat as though my impertinence had caused instant reflux. He reiterated, "Your book needs work." At which time, I smiled from the dawning realization that this scumbag hadn't read one page of the manuscript for if he had he would have known that there was no scene with humping camels as the beasts are not indigenous to Fallbrook, California. But then native New Yorkers have some queer ideas of life west of the Mississippi. Having faced the fact that I was playing a lost charade, I made no further effort to determine why he agreed to see me or why I had been brought to New York. My desire was to heap insults upon his ancestors until I was exhausted but it would have been to no avail. Top Dog was the type that thrives on insults. Said he, "We aren't taking on any new writers at this time but we will spread the word about your book. Perhaps some less prestigious agency might be interested. But we cannot promise anything."

Now with a blazing hatred for this parasite, I persisted. "If you were taking on new writers at this time would you be interested in my book?"

"But we are not," he reminded.

I smiled, in a manner to shatter glass, nodded to the spirit of Kafka who was with us, as I rose from my chair, swept my manuscript from the creep's desk and left without further word.

Back home on the Mojave, and recovered somewhat from my New York adventure, I made ready to drive into LA for an interview with someone named Rene' Rae who picked up on my book after about ten referrals which went through the usual Hollywood milieu. There was a certain comfort in knowing the area well and that I always come home from LA with a case of culture shock.

The Rae Agency occupies a suite in one of those cozy enclaves on outer Sunset, a middlingly respectable address that, architecturally speaking, combines the worst of hotel, motel and minimall rentals. Frank Lloyd Wright would be amused.

Rae's secretary was a black butch dyke who loathed me on first sniff. She seemed to suspect that I pick my nose in public. My four quick reactions to B.G. Pain, so indicated by nameplate on her desk were these: (1) B. G. was a remarkably handsome woman: (2) from a pair of short jodphurs cut from exquisite leather, tailored gray flannel slacks, blue blazer lined with red over a blouse of ivory silk she revealed excellent taste in clothes, all of it topped by a close-cropped Afro that was most becoming; (3) B.G. frightened me as I am sure that I saw her once on Roller Derby busily throwing bodies about and (4) B.G. was built like a decathalon champion with remarkable thighs.

I was barely seated in the outer office when B.G. dialed to announce, "He's here." Her words reenforced my feeling that B.G. did not like me or writers or both.

As we entered the office of Rene' Rae I was overwhelmed by a plethora of growing green flora along with her applied scent which brought me to a paroxym of sneezes. When the attack passed, Ms. Rae indicated a chair and said, "Dollingk, you heff a cold." Obviously, her Middle European accent gave Rene'Rae away as having started life as someone with a name like Hannah Lubinsky. Out of context, she laughed the first of her three ha-ha's that were flat and metallic in key and tone. Most disturbingly, when she laughs, her large nose turns downward toward her teeth. Grateful was I for dark glasses for I did not went Ms. Rae to suspect that the look on my face had nothing to do with allergies.

"Mr. Dunn, vud you like to smoke? Poisonally, I don't indulch." Silently, I said nay with a shake of my head as Rene' made the first of her startling gestures: hand to open desk drawer then up and over the desk and a sweep by her none followed by a sniff. Rene' smiled as though I had never heard of the White Stuff in good old Hollywood which is a Killing Field in itself. Gargled Rene', "Mr. Dunn, I am simply undone by your book. It's...smashingk!"

I gave thanks with a polite nod as I examined Rene' carefully, beginning with her hair. After years of bleaching her heavy black mop that which remained was a coarse substance somewhere between gray and white which was held together by a powerful lacquer. Her coif was swept back from her prominent forehead and came to an end in a modified Page Boy style. Her dress was cut from expensive satin of a mocha shade suitable for a soiree but not for any legitimate morning occasion. The neckline swooped down into a V and revealed more of Rene's mammalia than one wished to see. Instantly, I thought of Brian, a stalwart character from my book, a young Marine from Minnesota who allowed a barfly to buy him several beers and then felt that the honor of the Corps demanded that he bed her down. Brian is shocked at the sight of DeeDee's elongated breasts that remind him of rotting pears.

But back to Rene' who is large of frame and cadaverously skinny. Her long nails are held almost horizontally except when gesticulating and are painted in Revlon's newest shade called Dried Blood. "Vot mattidial, vot imaches! Ist all true or did you mek it up, you naughty boy." Rene' cackled lustily to indicate, so I assumed, that she was one of the girls or one of the boys, as the party might demand. I knew that my mouth had frozen half open or half closed, depending on whether one is an optimist or a pessimist, and I didn't know what to do about it, my mouth, that is.

Reluctantly, I forced myself to look at Rene's face and it was the eyes, the eyes that mesmerized me, those enormous agates of purple hue. The lids over her cavernous orbs resembled reconstituted toilet tissue generously smeared with mauve and white. So help me, some stardust had been touched to the outer edges for an eleven o'clock business appointment. The lashes! Well, anything that long had to be false. Only the load of mascara was real and gave to Rene' the appearance of a cayman looking for lunch.

The phone rang in B.G,'s office which caused me to shake. To cover my confusion, I took time to swab my burning nose with a tissue from my pocket. As I did, Rene' brought the Dried Blood nails in that startling arc past her nose and sniffed at the propitious moment. Hers was an ingenious way of getting the elixir into her hungry nostrils. I winced. And cursed myself for having written a book.

B.G. entered and gave me her most venemous glare as she approached the desk where she dropped a sheaf of open correspondence in some sort of marble receptacle that might have been a birdbath back in ancient Rome. At this point, Rene' placed the five claws to her right hand on B.G.'s ritzy blazer. Her's was the gesture of one who liked to flaunt their possessions. There followed her three metallic ha-ha's again and I suspect that she made the same sound when the Nazis shoved her grandmother into an oven. Meanwhile, B.G. continued to glare while I covertly marveled at her magnificent hams from behind my dark glasses.

"Mr. LaMarr on line two," B.G. explained, "Now! Or shall I have you call back?" Clearly, B.G. didn't think that I was worth missing a chat with the famous Mr. Swifty LaMarr, producer of hit movies. But I didn't have time to be insulted. I was consumed with worry about Rene's treacherous existence. Dining between B.G.'s powerful hams was indeed a way of living dangerously. Either in a state of ecstasy or in a state of pique, G. B. might snap those hams about Rene's head and crush her skull. Instantly, I had a morbid vision of Rene's crushed skull with hair broken into several pieces. I said to myself, B.G. is the type who likes to kill for her breakfast. As I did, Rene' pulled off the pearl earring clamped to her left ear, the kind that climb along the outer edge of the appendage, and grabbed another sniff of the coke all in one balletic movement. Receiver to denuded ear, she croaked: "Svifty, dollingk, how diffine of you to call." Svifty LaMarr had a lot to say and as he was saying it Rene' became more and more animated. As she did, the sweeps and arcs from coke to nose increased accordingly. If she kept at it, she would be stoned out of her black follicles before lunch, or so I assumed. All the while, she regarded my zipper which announces a budding gut. Apparently, Rene' is a switch-hitter, I decided. Wait until B.G. hears about that.

I drifted away from the telephone conversation, in a manner of speaking, until Rene' screeched: "Vot!" Her raucous voice made me think that she had a tropical bird somewhere behind her greenery. I shuddered politely. "Svifty, dollink, neffer could I handle dot fagula again. Last veek, I vent by his pless vid a fine script and found him in bed vid three boychiks... three yet!" Rene' frowned as I crossed my legs and I didn't know whether the rearranging of my body parts was the cause or whether Swifty LaMarr wasn't showing the proper interest in an actor with a penchant for young males. "Von day, Svifty, von day, dot fagula vill be caught." Rene' shivered deliciously at the thought. "Vot am I doingk? Vy dollink, I am gettingk acquainted vid a charmingk man who has written a fabulous book. Great vimmin parts. Fonda, Lange and Streep vud kill for soich roles."

Over my earthly remains, I raged, silently. When was the propitious time to tell these ghouls that none of the three mentioned actresses would ever appear in a film based on my book. If it can't be put in a contract then I'll burn the book.

"Ciao, Svifty, baby, tenks for cellingk and do invite me to lonch soon. I adore chili at Chasen's." Rene' disconnected...the phone, that is...and gurgled. "Svifty iss playingk it cool, dollink, but he iss verry interested to read your novel. It voss the great vimmin's parts that turned him on. Dollink, you write soich great roles for vimmin actresses." I didn't bother to inform Rene' that only vimmin can be actresses, except for Kabuki or for gays in drag. In fact, with B. G. riding shotgun on me, I was intimidated into a state of silence.

Finally, I said, "I admire strong women."

B. G. snorted and left us alone, as Rene' did her three ha-ha laugh for no apparent reason. "Dot vas Svifty LaMarr, dollink, the most sukkessful producer in diss crazy business. Perhaps he vill take us to Chasen's for lonch one day, after he reads your book." Her smile was more of a threat then an invitation, the kind that made me reflex too quickly in search of self-protection.

"Thanks, I've been."

"Been!" Rene' questioned my statement as her beaded lashes fluttered against her high cheek bones.

"To Chasen's."

"Oh!" Apparently, Rene' did not approve of unknown writers dining at her favorite restaurant which made me more obstinate that usual.

"How diffine, issen it," Rene' hissed.

Unable to control myself, I replied, "Personally, I found it highly overrated."

Something akin to color appeared on Rene's skeletal cheeks Obviously, she was displeased. Pushing my dossier around with one of her Dried Blood nails, she said, "You liff in Hemet. Ver is dot?"

"Near Palm Springs."

"But not in Palm Springsk?"

"Not quite."

"Dollingk, how can I do voik vid you ven you liff so far avay?"

"The telephone covers a lot of territory," I teased, and smiled as Rene' went for a sniff of the white elixir.

"Tell you vot ve are going to do, dollingk. You vill come to my pless for de veekend. Ve vill discuss your book."

Total recall of these two recent confrontations with agents played over and over in my head as though they were recordings that couldn't be stopped. Exhausted and numb from lack of sleep, I said: "This crap has got to cease." Rising from my rumpled bed, I went to my apothocary and took one of everything with a glass of my Dago red.

THE END

JARHEAD

Beware of calf-eyes that caress with long lashes. Be on guard against the young beguiler who comes too close too quickly. Remember that chameleons can be seen or not seen as they wish to be. Be not taken in by the intentions of youth which are as capricious as whirlwinds on the desert. Do not allow charm to dull a sense of danger perceived. Make a pact with your personal devils: refuse to fall under the spell of a timeless charade for which there is no win, only a murky solace for a sour place or show. Wiles and wit, experience and scars, jade and rote are insufficient weapons against the golden sorcerer. For those over thirty, time is your enemy, whatever your devils may argue; time is the young man's friend. Youth and your demons are hacking out an unholy alliance with yourself as the promised victim.

Stand tough against sudden rushes into intimacy; remember that you are the prey. Why lay it on the block no cheaply. One day met and on the next he is rearranging your life while the more he knows about you the less you seem to know about him. Senses are lulled by the euphoria of it. Reality is brushed aside as from a sedation. With high chagrin you find that you have volunteered to train him in the use of self-hypnosis so that he may kick the nicotene habit.

In addition to his Marine Corps duties, our diligent NonCom works at two additional jobs, or so he says. He lives off Base and drives a late-model car of Japanese make that is somewhat too expensive for a Lance Corporal's pay. Cynically, I decide that he's getting money from parents or from some other sources. Neat, clean and with manners impeccable, he arrives at my home for a session in hypnosis. At five-nine and one hundred forty-five pounds of muscle the young Jarhead is the quintessential All American boy for whom Moms and apple pies were invented.

You're the one to do it, my associate said, as he stroked me into working a shift with the new man who is a Marine. Who isn't in this town? They're all Marines, past or present. That began on a Tuesday, two weeks ago. Now, he walks in my steps, he is my new shadow. He is there to close shop with me and to sit in the back room and talk and drink beer while the electricity builds to a suffocating level.

Tours of the military installation are planned for my edification. His recognition of my oracular qualities is an opiate long denied. Oh, sweet elixir, he eats me alive with ravenous glances yet does not presume to touch. I become martyred meat to his psychological cannibalism.

Time takes on an aura of the surreal. On the day after his visit, even the beguiled has become aware of subtle fissures in his charming self, his oh, so marketable commodity. Queries commence as a preamble to mood swings toward the negative and the sullen. I am charged by dual emotional currents as I see two versions of himself. I begin to feel that I am an option to be traded rather than a flesh and blood entity.

One week has passed, one week since he first put his mark on me. "I really got to you," he chortles, as he arrives at nine and stays through the ten o'clock closing. We depart together. Outside, I find that his car is parked next to mine. He discovers that he has locked his keys inside. I could accuse him of premeditated contrivance but one has no proof. I drove him to his pad even though he lives but a short distance. He made an oblique reference to half a case of Heinekins in his frig as I parked in front of his building.

I eluded his invitation by saying, "It's a good beer."

He sat for a few seconds more and then mumbled, "Well, Tom…" as he got out and entered his living quarters.

I was informed that he was meeting his parents in Las Vegas come Friday as he made much of the fact that they were driving out to see him from the middle of Missouri. Due to his impending weekend trip, we scheduled an afternoon session in hypnosis for two o'clock. I was to continue on to work from his place. That I would have consented to this double duty makes me shake my head and ponder the measure of my sanity.

In my muddled emotional state I found an island of reason and came to terms with my needs: allergy shots are to be had on Thursdays and so I called the Jarhead and changed the schedule to Wednesday as he would be working only half a day, or so he said. On Wednesday, I called the allergy clinic to determine if they were to be open for business, Thursday being one of our quasi-holidays that clutter the calendar. I was informed that the clinic would be closed. Meanwhile, a friend mentioned the omnipresent: if I were to write two restaurant reviews for Le Rag, one of our local papers, eating out twice was a priority. Knowing that the All American boy had the day off, I called his apartment number at approximately ten o'clock hoping to juggle schedules.

A sultry secretary voice answered and I asked to speak with Kevin. In her officious and slightly odious manner, she wanted to know my identity, this from a young Marine's chick on the phone of a Lance Corporal who lives in a modest rental on the wrong side of the tracks. Gorge swallowed, I conceded to her demands. In a moment, a distant and possibly sleepy Kevin Morris took the phone. I made a cursory apology for having disturbed his rest, if that were the case, but the brown-eyed All American boy kept his response on the cool side as a gungho Marine should. I inquired as to his availability for a Wednesday session and he advised that he couldn't make it.

I managed to chuckle at the thought of Kevin's greedy little brain racing with plans to alleviate rising tension even though I was angry with myself for having fallen into such an obvious trap. This adolescent incident might be rife with implications and ripe with ramifications but to Kevin, charm can always soothe the savage beasts be they male, female, singular or plural. I knew further that he would make every effort to get to the store before the closing hour, which would be determined by his ability to dump the broad and if she were not dumpable then he would sneak out to a pay phone on one ruse or another. True to my predictions, Kevin did not show but called instead, five minutes before closing time, hoping to touch all bases. "Hi," he said, breathless with enthusiasm, "How you doing?"

I choked on his string of cliches but got them down without retort. "Working," I told him and, with malice aforethought, I asked, "To whom am I speaking?"

Agitation on the rise, he exclaimed, "This is Kevin."

"Kevin, how are you?"

"If you're not too tired and don't want to go home to bed, why don't you come by."

Having had his chick and having gotten rid of her, so I read the scene, he was now hungry for male companionship. When does this Jarhead sleep, I mused, as I spoke aloud into the receiver. "Thanks, Kevin, but I promised to meet friends in Vista for a round of drinks. I'll take a raincheck. If I may."

I felt the quake in his flat gut via the shake in his voice and was grateful for my innate ability to lie with conviction.

"Drinks in Vista, eh," he repeated, making the idea sound like the pits of boredom, "I'll see you later on," I had no idea what he meant as I rang off with a polite exchange thinking, as I did, that Kevin Morris was unaccustomed to being thwarted.

The following Tuesday became his first chance to see me after the trip to Las Vegas and he dashed inside around six o'clock which is a busy hour due to homebound traffic. Ill at ease and having lost his cool, he purchased two beers and I was aware of his efforts at self-control; the lines of strain around his mouth were easily detected by an old pro. Fortunately, I was busy and had no time to dally. By now, I knew that Kevin's life was a banquet and that he did not cater to having his eating habits disturbed. No mention was made of a session in hypnosis which I would have refused even if he had begged.

From this point forward I cannot recall exact time sequences in which the Corporal and I were involved but I do know that I did not see him for a week or more, except on a stormy night when I reached my street, a cul de sac in Oceanside, to find him parked near my house. Obviously, he was waiting for me to arrive, to check me out or to be asked inside but fear or indecision caused him to gun his motor as he sped away. Surely, he knew that I recognized him and his car.

On a cold and dreary winter evening, a plumpish young woman entered the store and asked if she might cash a small check for purchases. With proper identification, I agreed, having recognized her instantly by voice. She made too much of presenting to me her California Drivers License and her Military Identification Card which had been issued but a few days earlier to the wife of Lance Corporal Kevin Morris. I never saw her again. So much for a wedding in Las Vegas.

The seasons rolled around and on a scorching night in August I shared a Friday shift with my best buddy among the staff. Ten minutes before the closing hour, Corporal Morris entered the store wearing nothing but blood-red running shorts, courtesy of the Post Exchange, a Corps emblem guaranteed to reveal the best that nature has to offer. Expressing an overabundance of emotional duress, whipped up for the occasion, he announced that he had been assigned to a Marine contingent at Iwakumi, Japan and would be leaving soon. He whined about his fate, hoping to elicit sympathy and other goodies therefrom but my co-worker, and ex-Marine himself, extolled the virtues of such an assignment and assured Kevin that he would have a good time on his ten-month tour. I, too, got in the act and declared that travel can be broadening. These were neither the words nor sentiments that the Corporal came to hear. Deflated, flummoxed, Corporal Morris departed the premises in a forlorn state. I did not expect that I would ever see him again yet I kept watch on the front entrance for months to come. There was a finality to our brief encounter made more so by Kevin's words about his future plans upon his return from Japan, at which time, he would take a discharge and would return to his home town somewhere in the middle of Missouri.

In the zany environment of a raunchy liquor store from where I looked out upon a small country town filled with avocado groves, where Wetbacks and Marines came to me to buy their suds and cigs, time was bent out of shape as I assumed an illogical frame of reference. I may never understand why it was that time…my time, at least…was juxtaposed to reality. What I know is that I came to the store as a literary spy, took a deep breath, turned around and discovered that three years had slipped by, three busy and stress-laden years while I remained at the emporium to spirits. My reasons for staying so long had nothing to do with the fair, as the song goes, mine were spurious and self-indulgent. My research on the town and its folk was sufficient for the proposed work, sufficient to the point of over kill. Finally, there came a day when I admitted to myself that the scene had become an obsession and that my threats to quit were a form of mental masturbation.

There was much in my life to combat and the memory of my brief interlude with the Corporal was not a priority. I must have accepted his absence, finally, as fact and finished, for I ceased to watch the front door.

Avocadoland was into a cold and wet season, the kind of winter that gives growers ulcers. Floods and freezing nights were causing heavy damage. My six-hour shifts were boring in the dampness and chill of a barny store without adequate heating. Previously, I had cut my hours so that I might devote four days a week to the book which was demanding to get on paper. My shifts were limited to Tuesdays, Wednesdays and Thursdays by choice: cash receipts indicated that these were the slowest nights of the week. I would have cut back even more but there comes a point where employers begin to question one's value. As I couldn't bring myself to quit I tried to fit in with three nights a week as a token appearance. To this day, I marvel at how little most people notice behavior patterns of others.

As the dreary night progressed toward another Christmas I looked up from the register one evening and saw Corporal Morris standing about four feet from me on the customer side of the counter. I had not seen him enter, even though I was alone, an oversight duly registered. In his natty way...and Kevin was forever natty...he wore crisp khakis with a gray, black and yellow plaid shirt. As expected, whatever he wore appeared to be high fashion togs from a top label but it was not his apparel that grabbed me, it was the look of strain on his youthful face. Don't ask why I would look over my right shoulder at the wall clock but look I did as the clock registered the hour as 8:55 PM, and when I looked back the Corporal had disappeared, as in a sense that he was no longer there. Instead of shock or intrigue, this seemed to be a norm that left me calm and detached as I walked around the counter and stood in the open front doorway. Dutifully, I took note: there were no cars on the large parking lot and there had been no sound from a departing vehicle. Resolutely, I walked outside to check the east end of the building where it was my habit to park my wheels. Mine was the only car on the lot. At that precise moment, I realized that the Marine had not been there…not in the flesh…and that his manifestation was parapsychological in essence. As I am no stranger to precognition, telepathy, or any of it, I had no trouble in accepting his appearance. More importantly, I knew that mine had been a precognitive warning that the Corporal would appear soon. All this occurred in the space of a few heartbeats. I returned to my station behind the register and the evening passed.

Dispassionately, I thought about the appearance which was not the first and probably not the last of my psychic experiences: years earlier, I had my first precognitive dream from which I woke in a state of panic as I was being chased by communists. A few days later, I was offered a job as a writer for the Party which was active on the San Francisco waterfront. The job offer was more scary than the dream itself. From this and similar experiences I learned that we human creatures do send and receive messages and that I had been forewarned that the All American boy was back in town.

The manifestation by Corporal Morris happened on a Thursday night. On my four-day hiatus from the store, I thought little about the experience, which seems odd to me even now, but that's how it was, away from me and fatalistic; the Corporal and I were destined to meet again, it was part of our karma and I had no license to change destiny.

On the following Tuesday evening, I looked up from the register and saw that the Jarhead had arrived, although I neither saw nor heard him enter. In a perfunctory way, I glanced at the clock, even though I knew that the time was 8:55 PM precisely. He stood in the same spot and was wearing the same clothing and with the same self-serving look of perplexity on his youthful face. In a reverse sort of way, the image I saw on Thursday past was a film clip of a reality to come, one that was now in the process of happening. Precognition and reality had been reversed which is to be expected by those of us who deal with this sort of phenomena.

This time, there was no doubt about his finite presence as he was expected. He waited for my reaction just as he had done on the previous Thursday which had been a dress rehearsal for our confrontation now in the process of occurring. In my hastily chosen role, I made hand gestures to demonstrate my struggle to recall his identity and data about him. Had he been older and a bit wiser he would have scoffed at my pretentions as I said, "You are Kevin Morris and the last time we met you were leaving for Iwakumi for your final tour of duty. When you returned, so I seem to remember, you were to be discharged from the Corps. At that time, you planned to return to your home town in the middle of Missouri."

"I did," the Corporal replied, "But I didn't like it, so I reenlisted." At this point, the Marine went into his All American Boy sales pitch as he screwed his earnest face into a plea and said, "Tom, we've got to get together real soon. We have a lot of unfinished business to talk about."

Defensively, I stiffened as I felt his tentacles reaching out for me while at the same time I was impressed by his barefaced effrontery. As this moment came, I recalled acting lessons of yore and tried to mask myself with a look of disinterest and disdain in equal parts. Apparently, I was successful for I saw him prepare to whine and stub his toe but then he thought better of it and left the store. In his squeaky clean car he pondered his options as I would think that a dedicated chess player might do. I could tell, as both vehicle and occupant were brilliantly reflected in the glass to the open front door. Opting for a graceful retreat, as the better part of temporary valor, he started his car and drove from the area. I reached for the local telephone directory as the sound died away and with little effort I found a listing for both the Marine and his wife which told me that he had been back in town for six months or longer.

I suspect that the Corporal had bargained with the Corps for reassignment to his former post and that he slipped back into old haunts with ease. Only a few names, faces and serial numbers were different. I know that he passed the liquor store each day that he went to work which is the easiest way to get on Base and Marines are creatures of habit by training and experience. I was equally sure that he had never entered the store on one of my shifts which was graphic testimony to the fact that he knew I was a sitting duck for three nights each week. Then there was my car which was parked on the east side of the building. Were these less than sufficient data for his birddog mind then somewhere in his wallet there could be found a slip of paper on which I had written my home telephone number during the first week of our meeting. Fellow employees, as well, were there to answer any and all questions about my schedule or about anything else that they might know or surmise. To this consumate predator, I was a bird in an ungilded cage, a quality that made him a fine Marine albeit less that a trustworthy acquaintance. Having reasoned thusly I asked myself this question: what took him so long to make his move? I ruled out indifference but not from an ego frame of reference, and certainly not because of the lack of a cat-and-mouse syndrome for it is the nature of the cat to toy with the rat when the stomach is full, secure in the knowledge that the meal is available when appetite strikes. Unflattering though it may be, I saw myself as the mouse to the Jarhead's cat.

Gut reaction told me that my earlier rebuffs stung the All America boy in places heretofore unrecognized as fatal charm had given him no chance to learn about the reality of rejections. Before I came into his orbit, the Marine had grown accustomed to the omnipotence of charisma, although I doubt that he would categorize his behavior thusly, which led to my opinion that defeat was nothing more than a temporary setback for the killer instinct that he brought to the Corps and for which no further training was needed. Shaking it down, step by step, I reached this conclusion: the Corporal's calendar had been crowded upon his return from Japan and I had been relegated to cold storage until he ran out of bodies to quell. Clearly, I was a sure thing for three nights each week but a bird in the hand lacks the excitement of a bird in the bush. Having reached these inferences, I knew that his delayed appearance was a prelude to events to come and that he would, with military precision, pursue me to his inevitable end, for nothing stings so much as the one who got away.

This recognition of forthcoming events gave me the courage to reach down inside for a belated decision to resign so that I might flee from the artful conniver. On the following Tuesday, I broke my fixation and quit and with an assortment of colorful and obfuscating lies I eased myself out of a customary two weeks notice which was of little consequence in a crummy liquor store where clerks came and went with the regularity of customers.

Having fled my cage, as it were, I shall never know all the answers to the Marine's machinations and I should like to think that neither did he, but I am not sufficiently naïve to believe that. What I do know is that the Jarhead was trouble in a small package.

THE END

CAT

My first memory involves a large paper carton in which I found myself among a litter of kittens. We were without a mother, food or water and I suspect that we were still of a suckling age. The carton in which we moiled had been placed just outside a supermarket entrance and we were oohed and aahed a lot by shoppers as they came and went. What happened to our mother, I will never know. Perhaps she was killed by a car or was lunch to a stray coyote fresh out of the Orange County hills. Being born in Orange County, California means that most anything can happen and probably will but I was to be one of the fortunates, as fate decreed. One morning, this big-butted, bottled-blonde with tits forever thrust forward precisely at nine and at three o'clock, this emotional piece of baggage fell in love with the spot of white on my baby cat nose, lifted me from the box and with casual movements stuffed me between her ballon boobs where I rode precariously as she careened her rickety old station wagon in and around Harbor Boulevard.

Slightly dizzy was I when we finally reached what was to be my home for an indefinite period of time, a white-trash trailer park near the hills in good old Orange County. Her abode was one of those oval-shaped and small silver-colored trailers that looked much like a loaf of bread. I hasten to say that hers was not the worst and certainly not the best unit in the park but inside, it looked even worse than the exterior would suggest, for my new Mom was a sloppy one who let fall what might there to lie until she tripped over it. The interior odor…the eau de vie, as it were…was a combination of cheap cosmetics, perfumes, gargle, plus numerous body cleansers including several douche bags, all of it hanging in open spaces and all of it driving me into paroxyms of sneezes. There was another odor therein not at first identified by a small kitten but one who grew to understand that the source of this alluring miasma came from an erotic source.

My new Mom had a sunny disposition and hummed a lot, mostly some strange rock tune, but then she couldn't sing on key any better than most of the rock stars of that time and place.

What I remember most of my new Mom was a habit of chewing her bottom lip, a series of mouth motions that made her voluptuous lips resemble at the most a weeping vagina. I often thought that if Mom were to stand on her head she would look just as well as she did standing on two feet, a matter proved to my satisfaction on the day that I played cute kitty and rolled on my back with paws in the air, the better to have a good look at Mom's pulsating vagina surrounding by dark brown hair.

It took me but a short while to realize that Mom turned tricks for a living and for pleasure, for if anyone was ever psychologically and physically suited for their work, it would be Tillie Longjohn who had picked me out of a cardboard box in front of a Ralph's Market.

When a trick arrived, Tillie would place me in my oval bamboo box with a satin pillow and there I was supposed to stay while Tillie and customer rocked and rolled through numerous orgasm. Bless Tillie's heart, she always came with her partner, for there was pride in her work as well as an unquenchable sexual drive. At the peak of these orgasmic experiences, the silver-colored trailer would shake, rattle and rock until my bamboo bed would commence to slide across the quivering floor. At the conclusion of each trick, Mom would collect her fee and then she would kiss her departing johns goodbye. Tillie was indeed a polite and generous whore; all men who frequented her bed went away with their machismo enhanced.

On bad days and through lean weeks, when money was short, Tillie would share her chocolate chip cookies and breakfast cornflakes with me. Although I hated both, I would nibble and lap the milk from around the dreadful cereal just to show her how grateful I was.

Tillie was something of a pariah in our park for whoring without subtlety but she tended the sick and let dirty old men feel her crotch for free so residents of the park kept somewhat of a laissez-faire attitude, until a desperate day when Tillie brought home a nasty man. He was into S&M...and by this time, I hasten to add that being a smart female cat, I recognized all of the abbreviations attendant to human sexuality...and I enjoyed luxuriating on Tillie's bed after her hard night's work. The odor of raw sexuality turned me on and Tillie either had a seminal flow of avalanche proportions, or she actually wet the bed during her dozen or so orgasm during a twenty-four hour period. How I loved to roll in all those delicious sexual odors. But back to the bad john who came to call.

As he and Tillie galloped toward their mutual orgasmic states Mr. S&M decided to put a lighted cigarette to Tillie's quivering nipples, and for this sybaritic endeavor, I scratched his legs and was kicked across the tiny trailer. Kicking her cat and trying to burn her nipples aroused in dear Tillie a righteous indignation; she threw her electric iron at her trick which caught him dead center of his forehead and opened a gash that would brand him forever as a satyr. With all this caterwauling in full cry, many of our tackytown residents came out in flannel nightshirts and with hair in curlers to listen and to help and someone obviously called the police for the brave men in blue came and went, sending the wounded john to the nearest emergency and taking a handcuffed Tillie off to jail.

As daylight came and went, and as my wee stomach began to twitch from a lack of food, I commenced to wonder what my future might be. But we cats have nine lives and my second one seemed destined to include the slum landlady who owned our tacky trailer park. She appeared in a black Mercedes near noon, her limousine driven by a Mafia type who talked a lot on his cellular phone. After viewing the mess that was Tillie's home, she twitched her nose, this well-gowned and smartly-coiffed dame and, at that point, I decided to shake and to look petrified as I curled in my bamboo basket. I wasn't really cold, of course, but thought that the time had come to do a bit of acting. Act the part, as they say in show biz, convince the audience that you are an abandoned poor little pussy cat with yellow-green eyes and blue-gray coat of fur except for a tiny white spot on the tip of your cute little nose. Either the slum landlady fell for the bait, or else she was impressed by my performance, as she opened her enormous purse and stuffed me inside, except for my head, and that's how I was graduated from po-white-trash-trailer-park living to a three-storied mansion somewhere off Mulholland Drive.

My new Mom, better known to her staff as Madam, had a golden bell attached to my jeweled collar as there were countless rooms in that tri-storied house where a pussy cat could easily get lost. As a result, she called me Tinkerbelle for awhile, then switched to another name which I prefer to forget, as she referred to me as Peedle Poo and, after that, she switched from one to the other depending on her mood. In addition to ourselves, Madam had a staff of housekeepers, gardners, cooks, a come-and-go secretary, and then there was the butler. By this time, I knew that Madam was loaded and that I had hit the jackpot, residentially speaking. Madam and I had breakfast together in her bed, served by that prissy butler who made no bones about his distaste for cats. I grew accustomed to being served the best of pate in a stemmed crystal goblet, all of it equally as ostentatious as a certain catfood company's television spot. Quickly, I learned to do finicky, to eat a little and to turn away, a sure attention getter and one which got me rushed to the family veterinatian where I was x-rayed for possible hairballs. After that, I learned to do subtle, else I would find myself at the vet's for a series of shots which are not fun. In short, I learned quickly how to work the scene, as any smart pussy would do.

When Madam went for a drive, or on a shopping spree, I would ride above the rear seat there to be warmed by the sun as we drove through the miasma of bad taste otherwise known as Beverly Hills. On other trips, I would curl in the indenture above the dashboard and the windshield, there to do personal grooming which drove the Mafia type out of his alleged mind. Indeed, I became the bitch-smart nasty cat of my most favored dreams and the more of a pain I became the more Madam seemed to love me. Perhaps there was a valid reason for this state of affairs; Madam was a bitch of all bitches who ruled her fiefdom with an iron fist in the proverbial velvet glove. Perhaps we complimented one another.

The fly in my soup, the seed in my tooth, as it were, turned out to be the family butler. He was a prissy Brit with a revolting Midlands accent who swished and quivered his way making all except Madam and me totally miserable. If he caught me in the kitchen, where I liked to be, as the kitchen staff tossed me favored tidlies from time to time, he would curse me in his dreadful dialect and throw things in my direction. Once he threw a kife, which stuck in the wood of a cabinet door. Reading the tea leaves perfectly, I reasoned that either the Brit or I would have to go and that it wouldn't be me. Once when Madam was having a small group for dinner I was alert and tried to play dirty. Having found the proper schematic, I swished my voluptuous tail, walked through freshly iced cakes to be served as a dessert, sipped from the bowl of punch until I grew dizzy from the liquor therein and decided to swear off ere I fell in and drowned. In spite of my tinkling bell, and the screaming of the butler once he found pussy tracks in his dessert, I made my way to Madam's boudoir and slept it off while the party was occurring. Later, Madam chewed his ass, metaphorically speaking, for serving inferior store-bought pastries, and he swore to anyone who would listen that he would kill that damned cat.

Battlelines drawn, I sneaked up to the third floor and to the butler's quarters one morning and found nothing of interest in his room but some girlie magazines and an array of cheap colognes. In his bathroom, I stood on my hind legs, forepaws on the rim of the toilet bowl while I started at my beautiful reflection in the water therein, at which time, the wretch came in, picked my ass off the floor by my tail and tried to flush me down the loo. At that moment, my third life came to the fore. I turned a somesault and clinging to his shirt, I crawled up his chest leaving blood marks as I went, over his shoulders and down his back, at which time I ran like a Christian pursued by the lions all the way down to the second floor and into Madam's bed.

"Oh, you poor dear," Madam cooed, "Whatever did you do?"

At that point, the butler appeared, wet, sweaty and blooded by my strange safari up and over his shoulders. "Hah-rold," said Madam, in that strange pronunciation she gave to the butler's name, "Peedle Poo is all wet, wrap her in a towel and put her under my hair dryer to dry. And I mean dry, not roast."

Although Harold wanted nothing more than to squeeze my tiny neck until my yellow-green eyes popped out, he did as bade, for he knew that if he harmed a hair on my beautiful body the repercussions would be dreadful: Madam would pick up his Green Card and he would find himself on a cheap midnight flight to jolly ould England. I smirked at him a few times, secure in my exalted position, and I enjoyed the hair dryer immensely. But nothing was settled by my temporary victory for it was now a war unto the death between the butler and Madam's precious pussy. I was the undercat, pardon the pun, in a physical sense, but when it came to scheming brains, Harold was out of his league.

One of my favorite lounging places was on the top shelf of a rack that held spices, herbs and other sneezy things, and from my vantage point I could peruse all kitchen doings. My lolling lair was too high for Harold to reach, except with a stepladder and, with tail twitching, my contemptuous stare followed every move which drove poor Harold into paroxysms of rage. If he so much as sneered at me, I would howl as fiercely as my relatives do when they gather on a back fence during the mating season. Such cries led the staff to accuse Harold of mistreating me, a bit of news that the cooks and maids made sure was embellished by travel from the kitchen to Madam's boudoir. Thus was poor Harold hoisted on his own petard, so I heard the humans say, a phrase that sounds sort of sexy to me. At this juncture in our battle of wits, Harold grew careless.

On a lazy afternoon, near Madam's dinner hour, I observed as Harold prepared a tray for the lady of the house. Once the food was covered in its silver service, our Butler placed one white rose in a vase and in a crystal goblet he poured Madam a glass of champagne. In haste, and disregarding my baleful eye, he reached to the top shelf for a small vial of an unidentified white substance. As he took the bottle in hand, I raked my claws across his right hand drawing blood and yowls of dismay, rage and pain from the poor bastard's mouth. As he feared most Madam's wrath if her meal was overdue, Harold donned a white glove to make do. Back on his feet, as it were, I saw this mean man pour a bit of white substance into my mistress' glass of champagne.

During the following days, I watched as this routine was repeated daily. Before long, Madam became ill. Doctors, lawyers and other interested parties came and went as a hush fell on the house just off Mulholland Drive. I was not surprised when Madam was taken to a hospital and in my cat bones, I sensed that she would not be coming back.

After her death, the house and its occupants grew silent as officials came and went. Everyone was interviewed, except myself, of course. Then the news broke on tellie: Madam had been slowly poisoned by arsenic. More policemen and detectives came and went and the house was searched methodically. I was in my usual spot atop the kitchen shelves on the morning when Harold was given a polite third degree, meaning than none tied him aloft by his toes, an outmoded torture from ages past. At that point, I did not like the turn of events and with my dangling paw, I gently nudged the bottle of arsenic from the shelf. It fell to the floor with thud of doom, as Harold glared at me with a mixture of hatred and panic on his frightened face. The bottle rolled a bit toward a policeman's shoe and there it stopped. The cop reached down for the bottle which he passed to the detective in charge. At this point, poor Harold fragmented into a thousand shards and confessed all. He had, indeed, been feeding Madam arsenic for quite some time. His reasons for: he was under the hallucinatory impression that Madam had written him into her will and this bit of madness, fed by his gambling debts piling high led him into his deadly endeavor. Dear Harold was given a lifetime retirement at Folsom Prison where, I am happy to say, he will be buggered daily by one or more lovers not of his choice.

When the last will and testament was read to the gathered the silence was deafening. Madam left her entire estate, in trust, to her darling foundling pussy better known as Tinkerbelle and sometimes Peedle Poo. The trust was to be administered by Madam's favorite bank and a lover of cats was to be employed for the sole purpose of keeping a feline heiress happy. At the time of my demise the estate will pass to the Society for the Prevention of Cruelty to Animals where stray pussy cats such as myself will have the best that money can buy.

Currently, my keeper and I are touring the Mediterranean aboard Madam's yacht.

The End

DOG

My name was Hey U Jorge de Bernardo, so registered with the AKC, that august foundation that keeps track of pure-bred pooches like myself. The Hey U in my name referred to the kennel where my mother was born but she was not bred there. So pure was her lineage, so illustrious the kennel, so numerous the medals among my ancestors, all these variables led to my mother being flown to some place in Illinois there to be mated to one of equal stature much in the manner of royalty in centuries past.

The Hey U Kennels, where Dalmatians were raised exclusively, sat on a sprawling mesa among the mountains east of San Diego and it was there, in one of the many bedrooms, that my mother gave birth to a litter of six, aided and abetted by my human grandfather who bore the name of George and who, with his wife Lou and two male siblings, owned and operated the Hey U Kennels.

A few weeks prior to my birth, two dog-dumb males were referred to the Kennel, of a mind to own a Dalmatian. One of the two had grown up among dogs as his father fancied himself to be a hunter while the second of the two had never owned a pet. For these reasons, or so it seemed to me, my human grandparents took their own sweet time in deciding if the potential dog owners would be suitable parents to a prized Dalmatian. In casing the two in question, there occurred numerous visits and meals at the Kennel house, where beer, Scotch and other spirits flowed freely and where hearty ranch-style meals were consumed. In fact, my potential pack became good friends with George and Lou and waited patiently for my mother to deliver. Among the litter there were four females and two males, including myself and a brother who would be called Don Diego.

The final decision as to whether Don Diego or I would go home with the novice twosome…hereinafter referred to as the Dog-dumb Daddies One and Two…was left to human grandmother Lou who was a slender and quiet person and who was highly clairvoyant, so my Dog-dumb Daddy #1...hereinafter referred to as DDD1...often said. I didn't know what that word meant but came to understand that all dogs are that way, too, and my DDD1 would often speak of how he enjoyed watching my milky white aura as I slept near his feet while he stared at that silly box called TV. He told everyone who would listen how my aura would rise and fall from my body in a manner of quiet waves touching and receding from the shore. Eventually, I came to understand...in a dog way, of course...what being clairvoyant meant. When my DDD1 was upset or feeling poorly, I would get the colic, at which time, he would pour that nasty pink stuff down my throat until he got wise and put the pink pills in a meatball. When I had the colic, my stomach could be heard in full gurgle throughout the house. I came to understand that my DDD1 had a nervous stomach, also, and that he swilled Pepto-Bismol along with Scotch, gin and Courvoisier brandy. I came to understand that my DDD2 did not have a stomach problem and that gin was his panacea for all earthly ails. One day, he gave me a saucer of beer which I spat on the kitchen floor thus ending any and all speculations of my becoming a dogaholic.

Being a clairvoyant and being a dog is a double something or other in people language as all animals are...clairvoyant. Being a dog means that your nose knows when cheese is being unwrapped even though you're a block from the kitchen.

But back to my brother, Don Diego. We hated one another from the time our eyes opened. He wasn't as beautiful as I, neither was he as sensitive as I. When our human grandfather took us to a puppy show, I won a prize for show but my brother was judged the best for breeding. I viewed this decision as proof that Don Diego was a bit on the lower-class side in dogdom, although he was a regular stud, an on again, off again, thank you m'am breeding machine. When my grandfather tried to breed me to bitch Wanda, both of us still in a virginal state, she would sit down when I was ready and when she was prepared and receptive I became a nervous mess with a gurgling gut. As soon as we could control our streams, Don Diego and I pissed on each other whenever possible. When placed in adjacent kennels, all we did was to piss, piss and piss on each other until our bladders were dry. Had we been able to get at one another we might have pulled a Cain and Abel and pissed ourselves to death. I had the class but Don Diego had the balls for breeding, the lout.

DDD1&2 wanted to name me after my human grandfather but this was unacceptable to the American Kennel Club, so they chose to name me Jorge (Spanish for George) which was acceptable to the AKC. The de Bernardo in my name was legitimate as my pack lived in the community of Rancho de Bernardo at that time.

On the day that grandmother Lou made the decision to send me home with my new family, I tried to dig myself to China via a flowerbed on the front lawn but ten-week old pups cannot accomplish much. What happened is that I got muddy and was given a quick bath and wrapped in a towel and that's how I rode to my new home secure on DDD1's thighs. I remember becoming squirmy about the time that we reached the Poway High School campus and that's where I was let out, on leash, to peedle and poop. I felt secure with my new pack, those two dog-dumb guys, for it didn't take long for me to realize that they would become my slaves.

When we reached my new home my DDD's didn't quite know what to do with me. After some consultation, they spread pages from the San Diego Union on the garage cement floor and tethered me with a chain, as if a ten-week old pup was going to run away. I knew, even at that early age, that I belonged in the house as I was born house-trained, but I had no way to communicate this to my new pack. Instead, I did my best to do my do on the San Diego Union which was prophetic at best, although I didn't know it, for according to DDD1 and a few years later, the San Diego Union shit on him as their first restaurant critic. But I was destined to be a house dog and, in a short time, I had access to all parts of it, only to be put in a roomy cage for sleeping purposes.

We got along with this arrangement until I was six months old, which must have been in September, the time for the Santa Anas, the winds that blow westward from off the Mojave to sear the Southern California area. DDD2 slept in the master bedroom and on super-king bed which belonged to DDD1 who had abandoned the sumptuous equipment for a long boy twin in the smaller of the two-bedroom house. If this sounds peculiar then you must take into consideration that DDD1 is a writer and all writers are peculiar at best. And so my dotty pack member slept and worked in the tiny room as he claimed that the twin bed was more suitable to his back condition. As DDD1 often said, back pains are perhaps the least of a writer's problems and all writers are crazy or else they wouldn't be writers. I didn't know much about such things but as a growing dog I did know that DDD1 and I had special powers between us. On a night of scorching winds, the three of us slept fitfully as we waited for the heat and fury to die down, and around nine o'clock, so my pack said, I became fretful and began to whimper. Each of my pack came at different times to console me but to no avail. I knew what was wrong of course, but had no way to tell them. All I could do was whine and shake. Perhaps an hour after my problem began, DDD1 experienced a rare phenomenon. He became disturbed for reasons unknown, later he was to say that he felt that he was under a cloud, of sorts, a state of being with which he could not come to grips. In a way, so I was to hear him tell it, he felt that he was possessed.

Finally, and totally out of control, DDD1 rose from his bad, clothed himself with shorts, T-shirts and shoes, grabbed his wallet and keys, opened the garage and drove from our house. He was still a nicotine addict at that time, the dummy, and had a compulsion to go out for cigarettes which demonstrates his fragmented mental state as there were cigarettes in the house. Therefore, it was not the lack of a smoke that took him that back route to a 711 Store, the closest marketplace to our house, at that hour, an all-night facility near Poway Road. Once there, DDD1 purchased a pack of cigarettes but could not bring himself to return to Rancho Bernardo via the route he had come. The fixation was too powerful to control, and led by this compulsion, he drove Poway Road west to highway 395 and thence north to Rancho Bernardo. For the rest of the night, the three of us slept fitfully.

Around 0700 hours on the following morning, the phone rang and DDD2 answered. One of the siblings from the Hey U

114

Kennels told him that my human grandmother Lou suffered an aneurysm at approximately nine o'clock on the night just passed. She lived but briefly in an emergency section and her last words were: tell Jorge I love him. Shortly thereafter, I was let out of the cage for good and my first efforts were devoted to climbing my way onto the super-king bed.

My growing up was traumatic for the three of us. On one occasion, they put me in a kennel for a weekend as they had to make a business trip. At the kennel, I refused to ear or to perform the normal bodily functions. I caught a kennel cough and almost died. I was never put in a boarding kennel again. In my puppy days, my human grandfather took me to dog shows but the effort was too traumatic for me and I always came home with the colic and loose bowels. Dog shows were terminated. Once or twice, they left me at the Hey U Kennels while on other business trips. All I did was to piss on my brother and to return home with the colic. These experiences led to the inevitable conclusion that I was a one-pack dog and that my people could not afford to leave me, not even for a night.

A few months after the death of my human grandmother, Aunt Ginny came to call, as she often did. Still a navy nurse, at that time, she raised screaming poddles as an avocation. Nuestra madre de los peros, so DDD1 often called her, sat with us on the patio in a welcomed warmth from a winter sun. Although carefully watched, I was free to roam amidst the flowers and as far as the oleanders that marked the back side of our property, until such time as Aunt Ginny became disturbed by my uncertain gait. When I grew more unsteady on my feet, Auntie conjectured as to the possibility that I had eaten an oleander leaf or two, said plants being allegedly poisonous to dogs. When I could no longer stand erect, my Aunt Ginny screamed, "Is there a Fleet enema in the house?" There was and she did. In a professional manner, she gave me the business between two beds of flowers. Shortly thereafter, I ejected the cause of my dilemma. From the poop papers on the garage floor, I had torn off the San Diego Union logo and had swallowed it unchewed for there it lay, on the ground for all to see, now sodden and slightly discolored by its quixotic journey through my alimentary

115

canal. Looking back on that unusual occurrence, as DDD1 often did, he read the incident as being prophetic in essence, a precognitive warning of a bad relationship to come. Why I was driven to tear off and eat the paper logo is a matter that I could never answer. What I did was what my instincts told me to do. DDD1 spoke of it as part of the alchemy between dog and mankind. Nurse Ginny, DDD1&2 being alive and of reasonable sanity, will attest by affidavit as to the authenticity of the dog-shits-paper caper. After writing ninety-eight restaurant reviews for the Union, between November 1977 and June 1979, DDD1 quit cold turkey and brought suit against the Copley Press for expenses unpaid. In his Small Claims Court charge, he asked for two hundred dollars in unpaid expenses and received a settlement in the amount of three hundred smackers. As a result of that negative experience, DDD1 claims that he cancelled his reservation in Heaven as he could not tolerate the thought of being closeted with all those boring Republicans.

I grew up to become a showpiece of doggery. Whenever I walked down a street, admiring glances followed me. My regal bearing seemed to turn on all who chanced to pass me by. I carried my celebrity with elan. I bore my baths gracefully but offered no help. On the contrary, I would protest by becoming eighty pounds of limp dog. DDD1 would strip and would then place me in the shower with himself. I would be soaped with the finest of shampoos. I disliked most having my ears cleaned and would shake and thereby throw suds into DDD1's eyes. After the deed was done, I sort of enjoyed being rubbed down with a towel and being led onto the patio for the final drying. I glistened in the warm sun. Came the day when DDD1 grew careless and for that moment there I was, damp and free of restraints. Seeing a moment of a lifetime, as simultaneously DDD1 saw the error of his ways, I gave him the <u>look</u>, knowing that he could not reach me before the fact, as I gave vent to the forces of destiny. I fled to the plowed gray earth that was a flowerbed now stripped of greenery and there I turned ground like a salamander as I rolled and roiled in the sandy soil. While this happened, DDD1 stood helplessly by and laughed himself silly until my misadverture was complete, at which time I went

116

to him and let him hook the lead to my collar. At that point, he sprayed me with cold water until I glistened in the morning sun. It was a fine day.

Early in my maturity, I developed an anal gland problem and surgery was performed. I came home with a slightly reconstructed orifice but it worked well and there were no serious post-surgical complications as I learned to do my thing with my new equipment. This surgery was sort of like having a nose job on the wrong end.

As a young dog, who had been unable to perform as a stud, sexual urges beset me as I reached my potent years. One fine day, as DDD2 showed our residence to his father and stepmother, there I was in the middle of the super-king bed giving myself what DDD1 often referred to as a self-service fellatio. I didn't know what such a thing meant but from thereon, and with the least of provocation, or in the presence of guests, females especially, I would perform fellatio on myself with one leg sky high at one o'clock. One of DDD1's bridge partners came for early supper on a break between afternoon and evening bridge sessions, and while she was dining with plate in hand, I performed fellatio before her. This hard-bitten broad remarked that she didn't know that she was going to have a sex show with her dinner. Inevitably, when riding in our yellow station wagon, and with the rear section all to myself, the motion of the car drove me into paroxyms of fellatio. On these occasions, passersby would wave, scream and toot their horns as I did my thing up and down good old highway 395.

Dark days lay ahead for me and my pack. DDD2 had been with kidney stones for about ten years when one of the particles stopped his ability to void. Emergency surgery became necessary and DDD2 entered the Veterans Hospital at La Jolla for six hours under the knife. Prior to this emergency, DDD1 had become a student at Hypnosis Motivation Institute, satellite campus in La Mesa, a surburb of San Diego where he attended classes twice a week, one on a week night, the second on a Saturday morning. As he approached his hypnosis training he decided that he could work part-time at some uncomplicated and stress-free job from which he could earn the cost of his tuition.

As he knew foods, wines and spirits, he chose to become a liquor clerk for a few hours each week. The proprietor of the first liquor store to employ him turned out to be a megalomaniac/sociopathic ton of lard who would kill his mother for a buck. This unfortunate association was aborted after a short duration. The second liquor consortium for whom he worked was owned by a paranoid/schizophrenic too revolting to contemplate. His third employee ran a creepy liquor store in Solana Beach and although this employer was a sane and likeable person, the store sat near the ocean and was frequently socked in by fog. On some shifts, not one customer entered the premises. The essence of the place was a combination of Edgar Allen Poe mixed with the Adams Family. DDD1 had to flee in order to hang onto his sanity. In order to accomplish his departure, he coerced DDD2 into making a telephone call to the store owner during which DDD2 advised the employer that DDD1 had gone to Texas to bury his mother and to settle an estate. DDD1 had often told me that DDD2 was a willing although atrocious liar.

Intertwined amongst all these employment capers, DDD1 had, upon a dare, written to the San Diego Union and informed them that they were one of the few metropolitan daily newspapers without a restaurant critic and that he was qualified. Upon a dare, two samples of his work were sent for scrutiny and he was hired to become a restaurant critic for the Copley Press. The pay was niggardly and no expenses were given as the Union top dogs fully expected him to fall on his face thus ending the need for non-essentials such as a restaurants critic. Much to the paper's surprise, so DDD1 infers, he was a smashing success and an instant albeit incognito celebrity. Interestingly, the more successful DDD1 became, the more he was loathed by the Union, to the point that he was forbidden to frequent the premises of the paper for Quote he was attacking restaurants liked by members of the paper Unquote. As DDD1 had no desire to visit the Union, so he was prone to say, this transparent excuse covered but barely such reasons as the Union policy against celebrities on their staff and, quite probably, DDD1's ultra-liberal political stance. Even DDD1 could see humor in his being a contributor to such a Far Right publication. Twice during his tenure as a restaurant critic, DDD1 discovered that two food joints roundly scourged for bad cuisine decided to sue the paper and their critic for eight million dollars. He was never advised of this tempest by the paper, he found out by a circuitous method that the paper was pacifying the outraged restaurateurs with free advertising. DDD1 shrugged and said, so much for journalistic integrity.

But back to DDD2 and his kidney surgery which occurred in the early spring of 1978. In April, of that year, DDD1 went big-time and wrote two reviews per week until his day of resignation. In addition to caring for a convalescent and walking me three times a day, DDD1 had to eat out at least twice a week in order to have fresh grist for his culinary meal. In addition to, there were the two classes in hypnosis per week, plus at least eighteen hours a week behind the counter of the Happy Jug. This last of those liquor stores worked sat on a sandy corner in Fallbrook, where Main and Mission intersect. Disreputable is a classy word for that filthy, drug-ridden emporium to spirits which catered to Marines, past and present, to grove owners, Wetbacks and their coyotes, to whores pimps and sexual athletes of any and all gender persuasions, and where prostitution is a misnomer in a cruddy town where most everyone is anxious to give it away. My DDD1 was hooked from his first shift there, where liquor was sold to anyone with cash in hand. In one transcendental moment, he saw a Faulknerian saga in scope and depth, where citrus and avocados had replaced cotton and where Wetbacks had replaced Blacks. This occurred on Faulkner's one hundredth birthday, so DDD1 was prone to recall. On a Friday afternoon, and with a flash of cognizance, he saw the Wetbacks marching to town, one line on either side of the street, as they made their weekly pilgrimage to the post office where dollars would be exchanged for money orders destined for <u>las</u> <u>familias</u> <u>en</u> <u>Mejico</u>. With the smell of sweat from <u>los</u> <u>trabajadores</u> fresh upon him, DDD1 knew that he was destined to write about the Fallbrook scene. He then complicated his life further by beginning a year of research into the history of North San Diego County and the coming of the Marines to the Mesa Margarita,

119

better known as Camp Pendleton. What exhausted DDD1 the most during his three years at the Happy Jug was not the fact that he was a literary spy doing undercover work for a book, and not the fact that he was a two-a-week incognito restaurant critic, what really turned him into putty were the frequent assignations that occurred in that dinky little wine cellar at the Happy Jug. LAND OF THE GREEN GOLD was finished eleven years and five surgeries later.

Somewhere in all this human activity, I developed kidney failure, a weakness among Dalmatians, so my pack and I learned. When our veterinarian gave up on trying to save me, my pack put me on 1000 IU's of Vitamin E per day. They told me they were cookies, but what the hell, they were tasty and so I wolfed them down with gusto. In time, a miracle of miracles occurred. My kidney failure was reversed. I ate some awful low-protein food during that time but I knew that my pack was trying to save my life. The bond between us grew deeper.

There came a day when my pack went to the Veterans Hospital as DDD1 was in need of urgent care. Sans appointment, he was subjected to an eight-hour wait which weighed heavily on their minds as I would be left alone without my customary afternoon walk. When they returned, late in the afternoon, they found me sleeping on the long-boy twin in DDD2's bedroom. What confounded them the most was the fact that I had gotten between the sheets and slept with my head on the pillow. As I came awake, I blinked and my tail gave a welcoming thump under the covers. I was perfectly all right, of course, as I went into hibernation and stayed there until my pack returned. They never did figure out how I managed to get between the sheets in such a neat manner. Firstly, I was a neat dog and, secondly, we pooches adopt the habits of our pack.

During my young adult years, we moved to the town of Vista. I didn't care where I lived as long as I was with my pack but I could feel the stress felt by them, a state generated by their dislike with their apartment building in which we lived. DDD1 played duplicate bridge during those years, which was an escape from writing, and he was at best a mediocre player as he would start writing in his head and forget what cards had been played which made him less than a desired partner. Fortunately, he came to his senses eventually and gave up this stupid game for more productive pursuits, such as writing novels, which is a non sequitur for sure. On the afternoon that DDD1 was to make his debut as an ACBL Director, he shaved his dome with a safety razor and then dressed for the momentous occasion, his drag consisting of a silken white shirt littered with red polkadots, his slacks the latest in sailcloth white, while his feet were shod in a pair of K-Swiss shoes, the latest in yuppie footwear. As his last task before leaving for the Bridge Center, DDD1 removed the used razor blade from the shaver and tucked it inside of an empty soap wrapper. As fate dealt the cards, he walked toward the kitchen and as he did, he crunched the soap carton, and knew instantly what he had done as blood spurted onto his chosen attire. At the kitchen sink, he ran water on his ruined left thumb and thought, vaguely, about his predicament. In shock, of course, he asked an eighty year old lady to drive him to the Oceanside Hospital instead of calling 911 for emergency service. The dear lady did her thing, at twenty miles per hour and, eventually, she deposited DDD1 at the entrance to ER with his left hand wrapped in a bloody towel. He checked himself in and sat down, at which time he informed the nurse that he was going to faint. With encouragement, she suggested that he put his head between his knees. Ultimately, the decision was made: the attending physician preferred to let the wound heal and to perform surgery later.

After surgery, DDD1 came home with bandages and a sling for his damaged appendage. This drove me into a frenzy as I was supposed to heal his wound with my tongue. Each time that I touched the wounded finger, DDD1 would scream. Eventually, I was locked out of the master bedroom to which I took umbrage in high dog style as it was my duty to take care of a wounded pack member.

Eventually, we moved to Oceanside and lived near Mission San Luis Rey. I had lots of interesting places to walk as there were vacant lots nearby and below them the San Luis Rey River. Wetbacks lived in the hills above our area and we often saw them on our walks but DDD1 made certain that we did not

121

invade their territory. On one frosty morning, with DDD1 half awake, of course, we turned a corner onto a deserted area and, voila, ahead of us stood three coyotes waiting for a confrontation. At this point, DDD1 came fully awake and said, "Jorge, let's get out of here."

At times, we broke the monotony of traveling the same territory on our daily walks and on such occasions DDD1 took me to a park in Oceanside frequented by joggers and dogs doing their morning bit. The Porvo II epidemic was upon us, at that time, and it must have been in that park where I caught this dreadful disease. I was ill when we moved to Hemet and a short while later my pack learned that I could not survive without the Porvo serum. On one long and painful weekend, they called every place in southern California where the serum might have been found but to no avail. There was simply none available. A local veterinarian filled me with liquids that would make my terminal illness as painless as possible. On the afternoon of my final day, I rose on unsteady feet and went to the front door with a silent request to be set free. My pack obliged, and as I stumbled about the yard, they sat on the cool cement of the garage floor mute in their grief as there was no way that they could save me, and it was toward them that I made my final journey. Once there, I laid my head on DDD2's thigh as I took leave of my body.

My pack was in shock, so I observed from the other side, for my passing was the first deep grief that either had ever experienced. When it came to removing my body, DDD1 simply could not do it. DDD2 showed a strength of character when he wrapped me in a towel and took me to a vet's office where he layed me on the trash behind the building. His last heroic act was to remove the chain that I had worn for all of my life. DDD1 had tickets for the Santa Fe Opera season, purchased so that he could see five operas in five nights, which only an opera freak could do. He canceled his flight and he and DDD2 drove to Santa Fe which was a good thing to do.

Even after moving to Hemet, DDD1 continued to work at the Fallbrook liquor store for three nights a week as it was there that he found the inspiration and characters for his novel called

LAND OF THE GREEN GOLD. Their despair over my passing was not a thing that would pass lightly and from the other side, I watched them struggle with their loss. The sight of my ball, my dry water bowl, white hairs on the carpet, in myriad ways I was never to be forgotten. Meanwhile, I stayed nearby, at one of two dairies and ranches near the stop-in-the-road known as Winchester, the road taken by DDD1 as he returned to Hemet after a shift at the liquor emporium in Fallbrook. Knowing precisely just when DDD1 would drive past that flat stretch of ground I did, on two occasions, perform the ectoplasmic bit: I dashed across Winchester Road in full view of the headlights on the Nissan wagon that DDD1 drove. He saw me, and knew that I was running with the horses which is in my genes, and he received the message that it was all right to let me go. Many years have passed and my pack still finds it difficult to look at photographs of me. I will always be the love of their lives and they will always be the loves in my life, that one that we shared together. I walk with my human grandmother Lou and all is well with us. Who knows, perhaps we will all be together in another time and place.

THE END

About the Author

Emmett Shields is a free lance writer currently residing in Barstow, California. Formerly, he was a restaurant critic for the San Diego Union. As a writer, a professional hypnotist and a clairvoyant, he declares that "What goes on in my head is the stuff that keeps psychiatrists in the upper income bracket." In spite of a busy writing schedule, he manages to remain active in para-psychological research.